Butson, Thomas G.   J
                           943

Ivan the terrible

IVAN
THE
TERRIBLE

IVAN THE TERRIBLE

Thomas Butson

CHELSEA HOUSE PUBLISHERS
NEW YORK
NEW HAVEN   PHILADELPHIA

EDITOR-IN-CHIEF: Nancy Toff
EXECUTIVE EDITOR: Remmel T. Nunn
MANAGING EDITOR: Karyn Gullen Browne
COPY CHIEF: Perry Scott King
ART DIRECTOR: Giannella Garrett

Staff for IVAN THE TERRIBLE:

SENIOR EDITOR: John W. Selfridge
ASSISTANT EDITORS: Maria Behan, Pierre Hauser, Kathleen McDermott, Bert Yaeger
COPY EDITORS: Gillian Bucky, Sean Dolan
DESIGN ASSISTANT: Jill Goldreyer
PICTURE RESEARCH: Toby Greenberg
LAYOUT: Teresa Clark
PRODUCTION COORDINATOR: Alma Rodriguez
COVER ILLUSTRATION: Fran Oelbaum

CREATIVE DIRECTOR: Harold Steinberg

Frontispiece courtesy of Roger-Viollett

First Printing

Library of Congress Cataloging in Publication Data

Butson, Thomas G. IVAN THE TERRIBLE

(World leaders past & present)
Bibliography: p. 108
1. Ivan IV, Czar of Russia, 1530–1584—Juvenile literature.
2. Soviet Union—Kings and rulers—Biography—Juvenile
literature. [1. Ivan IV, Czar of Russia, 1530–1584. 2. Kings,
queens, rulers, etc.] I. Title. II. Series.
DK106.B88   1987   943'.043'0924 [B] 86-30992

ISBN 0-87754-534-0

Contents

ADENAUER
ALEXANDER THE GREAT
MARC ANTONY
KING ARTHUR
ATATÜRK
ATTLEE
BEGIN
BEN-GURION
BISMARCK
LÉON BLUM
BOLÍVAR
CESARE BORGIA
BRANDT
BREZHNEV
CAESAR
CALVIN
CASTRO
CATHERINE THE GREAT
CHARLEMAGNE
CHIANG KAI-SHEK
CHURCHILL
CLEMENCEAU
CLEOPATRA
CORTÉS
CROMWELL
DANTON
DE GAULLE
DE VALERA
DISRAELI
EISENHOWER
ELEANOR OF AQUITAINE
QUEEN ELIZABETH I
FERDINAND AND ISABELLA
FRANCO

FREDERICK THE GREAT
INDIRA GANDHI
MOHANDAS GANDHI
GARIBALDI
GENGHIS KHAN
GLADSTONE
GORBACHEV
HAMMARSKJÖLD
HENRY VIII
HENRY OF NAVARRE
HINDENBURG
HITLER
HO CHI MINH
HUSSEIN
IVAN THE TERRIBLE
ANDREW JACKSON
JEFFERSON
JOAN OF ARC
POPE JOHN XXIII
LYNDON JOHNSON
JUÁREZ
JOHN F. KENNEDY
KENYATTA
KHOMEINI
KHRUSHCHEV
MARTIN LUTHER KING, JR.
KISSINGER
LENIN
LINCOLN
LLOYD GEORGE
LOUIS XIV
LUTHER
JUDAS MACCABEUS
MAO ZEDONG

MARY, QUEEN OF SCOTS
GOLDA MEIR
METTERNICH
MUSSOLINI
NAPOLEON
NASSER
NEHRU
NERO
NICHOLAS II
NIXON
NKRUMAH
PERICLES
PERÓN
QADDAFI
ROBESPIERRE
ELEANOR ROOSEVELT
FRANKLIN D. ROOSEVELT
THEODORE ROOSEVELT
SADAT
STALIN
SUN YAT-SEN
TAMERLANE
THATCHER
TITO
TROTSKY
TRUDEAU
TRUMAN
VICTORIA
WASHINGTON
WEIZMANN
WOODROW WILSON
XERXES
ZHOU ENLAI

ON LEADERSHIP
Arthur M. Schlesinger, jr.

LEADERSHIP, it may be said, is really what makes the world go round. Love no doubt smooths the passage; but love is a private transaction between consenting adults. Leadership is a public trans-action with history. The idea of leadership affirms the capacity of individuals to move, inspire, and mobilize masses of people so that they act together in pursuit of an end. Sometimes leadership serves good purposes, sometimes bad; but whether the end is benign or evil, great leaders are those men and women who leave their personal stamp on history.

Now, the very concept of leadership implies the proposition that individuals can make a difference. This proposition has never been universally accepted. From classical times to the present day, eminent thinkers have regarded individuals as no more than the agents and pawns of larger forces, whether the gods and goddesses of the ancient world or, in the modern era, race, class, nation, the dialectic, the will of the people, the spirit of the times, history itself. Against such forces, the individual dwindles into insignificance.

So contends the thesis of historical determinism. Tolstoy's great novel *War and Peace* offers a famous statement of the case. Why, Tolstoy asked, did millions of men in the Napoleonic wars, denying their human feelings and their common sense, move back and forth across Europe slaughtering their fellows? "The war," Tolstoy answered, "was bound to happen simply because it was bound to happen." All prior history predetermined it. As for leaders, they, Tolstoy said, "are but the labels that serve to give a name to an end and, like labels, they have the least possible connection with the event." The greater the leader, "the more conspicuous the inevitability and the predestination of every act he commits." The leader, said Tolstoy, is "the slave of history."

Determinism takes many forms. Marxism is the determinism of class. Nazism the determinism of race. But the idea of men and women as the slaves of history runs athwart the deepest human instincts. Rigid determinism abolishes the idea of human freedom—

the assumption of free choice that underlies every move we make, every word we speak, every thought we think. It abolishes the idea of human responsibility, since it is manifestly unfair to reward or punish people for actions that are by definition beyond their control. No one can live consistently by any deterministic creed. The Marxist states prove this themselves by their extreme susceptibility to the cult of leadership.

More than that, history refutes the idea that individuals make no difference. In December 1931 a British politician crossing Park Avenue in New York City between 76th and 77th Streets around 10:30 P.M. looked in the wrong direction and was knocked down by an automobile—a moment, he later recalled, of a man aghast, a world aglare: "I do not understand why I was not broken like an eggshell or squashed like a gooseberry." Fourteen months later an American politician, sitting in an open car in Miami, Florida, was fired on by an assassin; the man beside him was hit. Those who believe that individuals make no difference to history might well ponder whether the next two decades would have been the same had Mario Constasino's car killed Winston Churchill in 1931 and Giuseppe Zangara's bullet killed Franklin Roosevelt in 1933. Suppose, in addition, that Adolf Hitler had been killed in the street fighting during the Munich *Putsch* of 1923 and that Lenin had died of typhus during World War I. What would the 20th century be like now?

For better or for worse, individuals do make a difference. "The notion that a people can run itself and its affairs anonymously," wrote the philosopher William James, "is now well known to be the silliest of absurdities. Mankind does nothing save through initiatives on the part of inventors, great or small, and imitation by the rest of us—these are the sole factors in human progress. Individuals of genius show the way, and set the patterns, which common people then adopt and follow."

Leadership, James suggests, means leadership in thought as well as in action. In the long run, leaders in thought may well make the greater difference to the world. But, as Woodrow Wilson once said, "Those only are leaders of men, in the general eye, who lead in action. . . . It is at their hands that new thought gets its translation into the crude language of deeds." Leaders in thought often invent in solitude and obscurity, leaving to later generations the tasks of imitation. Leaders in action—the leaders portrayed in this series—have to be effective in their own time.

And they cannot be effective by themselves. They must act in response to the rhythms of their age. Their genius must be adapted, in a phrase of William James's, "to the receptivities of the moment." Leaders are useless without followers. "There goes the mob," said the French politician hearing a clamor in the streets. "I am their leader. I must follow them." Great leaders turn the inchoate emotions of the mob to purposes of their own. They seize on the opportunities of their time, the hopes, fears, frustrations, crises, potentialities. They succeed when events have prepared the way for them, when the community is awaiting to be aroused, when they can provide the clarifying and organizing ideas. Leadership ignites the circuit between the individual and the mass and thereby alters history.

It may alter history for better or for worse. Leaders have been responsible for the most extravagant follies and most monstrous crimes that have beset suffering humanity. They have also been vital in such gains as humanity has made in individual freedom, religious and racial tolerance, social justice and respect for human rights.

There is no sure way to tell in advance who is going to lead for good and who for evil. But a glance at the gallery of men and women in *World Leaders—Past and Present* suggests some useful tests.

One test is this: do leaders lead by force or by persuasion? By command or by consent? Through most of history leadership was exercised by the divine right of authority. The duty of followers was to defer and to obey. "Theirs not to reason why,/ Theirs but to do and die." On occasion, as with the so-called "enlightened despots" of the 18th century in Europe, absolutist leadership was animated by humane purposes. More often, absolutism nourished the passion for domination, land, gold and conquest and resulted in tyranny.

The great revolution of modern times has been the revolution of equality. The idea that all people should be equal in their legal condition has undermined the old structure of authority, hierarchy and deference. The revolution of equality has had two contrary effects on the nature of leadership. For equality, as Alexis de Tocqueville pointed out in his great study *Democracy in America*, might mean equality in servitude as well as equality in freedom.

"I know of only two methods of establishing equality in the political world," Tocqueville wrote. "Rights must be given to every citizen, or none at all to anyone . . . save one, who is the master of all." There was no middle ground "between the sovereignty of all and the absolute power of one man." In his astonishing prediction of 20th-century totalitarian dictatorship, Tocqueville explained how the revolution of equality could lead to the *"Führerprinzip"* and more terrible absolutism than the world had ever known.

But when rights are given to every citizen and the sovereignty of all is established, the problem of leadership takes a new form, becomes more exacting than ever before. It is easy to issue commands and enforce them by the rope and the stake, the concentration camp and the *gulag.* It is much harder to use argument and achievement to overcome opposition and win consent. The Founding Fathers of the United States understood the difficulty. They believed that history had given them the opportunity to decide, as Alexander Hamilton wrote in the first Federalist Paper, whether men are indeed capable of basing government on "reflection and choice, or whether they are forever destined to depend . . . on accident and force."

Government by reflection and choice called for a new style of leadership and a new quality of followership. It required leaders to be responsive to popular concerns, and it required followers to be active and informed participants in the process. Democracy does not eliminate emotion from politics; sometimes it fosters demagoguery; but it is confident that, as the greatest of democratic leaders put it, you cannot fool all of the people all of the time. It measures leadership by results and retires those who overreach or falter or fail.

It is true that in the long run despots are measured by results too. But they can postpone the day of judgment, sometimes indefinitely, and in the meantime they can do infinite harm. It is also true that democracy is no guarantee of virtue and intelligence in government, for the voice of the people is not necessarily the voice of God. But democracy, by assuring the right of opposition, offers built-in resistance to the evils inherent in absolutism. As the theologian Reinhold Niebuhr summed it up, "Man's capacity for justice makes democracy possible, but man's inclination to injustice makes democracy necessary."

A second test for leadership is the end for which power is sought. When leaders have as their goal the supremacy of a master race or the promotion of totalitarian revolution or the acquisition and exploitation of colonies or the protection of greed and privilege or the preservation of personal power, it is likely that their leadership will do little to advance the cause of humanity. When their goal is the abolition of slavery, the liberation of women, the enlargement of opportunity for the poor and powerless, the extension of equal rights to racial minorities, the defense of the freedoms of expression and opposition, it is likely that their leadership will increase the sum of human liberty and welfare.

Leaders have done great harm to the world. They have also conferred great benefits. You will find both sorts in this series. Even "good" leaders must be regarded with a certain wariness. Leaders are not demigods; they put on their trousers one leg after another just like ordinary mortals. No leader is infallible, and every leader needs to be reminded of this at regular intervals. Irreverence irritates leaders but is their salvation. Unquestioning submission corrupts leaders and demands followers. Making a cult of a leader is always a mistake. Fortunately hero worship generates its own antidote. "Every hero," said Emerson, "becomes a bore at last."

The signal benefit the great leaders confer is to embolden the rest of us to live according to our own best selves, to be active, insistent, and resolute in affirming our own sense of things. For great leaders attest to the reality of human freedom against the supposed inevitabilities of history. And they attest to the wisdom and power that may lie within the most unlikely of us, which is why Abraham Lincoln remains the supreme example of great leadership. A great leader, said Emerson, exhibits new possibilities to all humanity. "We feed on genius. . . . Great men exist that there may be greater men."

Great leaders, in short, justify themselves by emancipating and empowering their followers. So humanity struggles to master its destiny, remembering with Alexis de Tocqueville: "It is true that around every man a fatal circle is traced beyond which he cannot pass; but within the wide verge of that circle he is powerful and free; as it is with man, so with communities."

1

The Boy Tsar

As the men crashed through the door to Ivan's bedroom, the 11-year-old grand duke of Moscow, shocked out of his sleep, sat bolt upright in bed. With his heart pounding and his nerves stretched taut, Ivan fought to hold back the terror he felt at the sight of the group of boyars (the nobles of medieval Russia) standing before him.

The boyars' midnight raid on the priest's residence had very nearly succeeded. But Metropolitan Joseph, the head of the Orthodox church in Moscow and a vocal supporter of the rival Belsky family, had fled to the royal quarters at the Kremlin at the last minute. The boyars had pursued Joseph this far, however, and were determined to bring him back. They had hesitated outside Ivan's door for only a moment. They had, after all, sworn loyalty to him, but they knew that they would find only a withdrawn, rather nervous boy inside.

Convinced that he was about to die, Ivan strained to recognize the men in the faint light of early dawn. His small, somber gray eyes darted across the bo-

> *By nature the tsar is like any other man, but in power and office he is like the highest God.*
> —Muscovite church council, 1504

Ivan IV, son of the grand duke of Moscow, was the first Russian ruler to crown himself tsar, in 1547. Ivan brought to an end the feudal political order of medieval Russia through the establishment of a centralized Muscovite autocracy.

Grand Duke Vasili III, Ivan's father. During Vasili's reign Moscow extended its authority over the surrounding region and adopted the title of the "Third Rome" as the center of the Orthodox Christian world.

yars' faces, and his quick mind registered names: these were Shuisky's men. As the nobles searched the room, the young prince tried to speak, but fear held him fast. When the boyars discovered that the metropolitan was not hiding in the boy's chambers, they threw a last look of contempt at the terrified Ivan and left to continue their search. Ivan stared at the open door for a long time.

For years Ivan had watched as factional struggles among the great boyar families had led to destruction, bloodshed, and near anarchy in Moscow. The boyars had ignored, manipulated, and humiliated Ivan since the death of his mother, the regent, four years earlier. Now they had terrorized him. Disgust and rage at the arrogant, greedy boyars burned into Ivan. He would not forget.

By the reign of Grand Duke Vasili III in the early 1500s, the grand duchy of Moscow had undergone phenomenal change. The princes of Moscow had transformed the area from an insignificant community, one of the many local independent principalities that made up medieval Russia, into the dominant political power of the region. The old *appanage* political order of separate, autonomous communities, each with its own local hereditary lord, was in its death throes. A new order, a unified state under the central authority of Moscow, had arisen.

In addition to its political growth, Moscow had fallen heir to a crucial religious importance. With the fall of Constantinople (modern Istanbul), the capital of the Byzantine, or Eastern Roman, Empire, to the Muslim Ottoman Turks in 1453, Moscow became the self-proclaimed leader of Orthodoxy, or Eastern Christianity, and thus successor to the Byzantine emperors. In the Orthodox tradition, Constantinople (built by Roman Emperor Constantine the Great in the early 4th century A.D.) had been the "Second Rome" — its rulers shouldering the responsibility of leading and protecting Orthodox Christians — after Rome fell to barbarian invaders in the 5th century A.D. During the reign of Vasili III, Moscow assumed this mantle of leadership as the "Third Rome," which, in the Orthodox literature, was the final stage before Judgment Day, when it was believed Christ would return to judge mankind.

The Muscovite rulers, members of what is known as the Rurik dynasty, thus acquired a political standing and a religious prestige that they used as justification for expansion in all directions. The duchy had nearly quadrupled in size by the end of Vasili's reign, in 1533. Moscow had seized many of the surrounding territories, including Rostov, Tver (now Kalinin), Ryazan, and Novgorod by force, while some communities, seeing the advantages of Muscovite protection and aiming to increase their own standing, voluntarily offered to enter the service of Moscow's rulers.

> *The apostolic church . . . stands no longer in Rome or in Constantinople, but in the blessed city of Moscow.*
> —PHILOTHEUS
> Pskovian monk, in a letter
> to Vasili III

When Grand Duke Vasili died in 1533, he left the now expanded state of Muscovy to his eldest son, Ivan. But Ivan was a child — he was born on August 25, 1530 — and his mother, Yelena Glinskaya, became regent. Yelena, together with a selected group of boyars, would rule Moscow until Ivan came of age to assume power. The other members of her powerful family, the Glinskys, rallied around Yelena, determined to keep all the power in the hands of their family. Princess Yelena, however, was not accustomed to wielding authority, and she relied heavily at first on one uncle, Prince Mikhail Glinsky. He

A group of boyars, the Russian medieval nobility, with the Kremlin in the background. When Vasili died in 1533, leaving three-year-old Ivan as heir, the boyars saw an opportunity to reassert their power in Moscow.

soon fell out of favor and was thrown into prison, where he died. After that, the princess left state matters largely in the hands of her lover, Prince Ivan Telepnev-Obolensky. She also shocked Moscow by refusing to follow custom and remain in the *terem* — the section of the royal palace where women were kept apart from men.

Without the strong presence of Vasili, who had kept the ambitions of the formerly independent boyars in check, a power struggle among the noble families erupted. The great nobles of Moscow, who were jealous of the Glinskys, plotted their overthrow. After five years of turmoil, they succeeded. Princess Yelena died, possibly of poison, on April 3, 1538. With her death, Obolensky soon lost his power, and Yelena's two young sons, Ivan and Yuri, became the focus of a raging political battle.

Because Ivan himself was still too young to rule, Moscow's government passed into the hands of the boyars. While the noblemen fought personal and family battles among themselves, the central administration that Ivan's father, Vasili, and grandfather Ivan III had built in Moscow began to deteriorate.

Among the boyars, two great families, the Shuiskys and the Belskys, competed for supremacy. Power changed hands several times, and Moscow slid toward anarchy. Murders, imprisonments, and executions were commonplace. It seemed that no one was safe. Even Metropolitan Joseph finally fell victim to the factional fighting. Eventually, after years of violent feuding, the Shuiskys prevailed, but their rule, aimed only at increasing their own wealth and power, proved no blessing for Moscow and especially not for young Ivan.

The Shuiskys were responsible for Ivan's upbringing and, ironically, for the young prince's safety. Ivan and his brother became pawns of the boyar family. Years later, Ivan wrote of one incident involving Andrei Shuisky, who had been regent: "I recall how the boyars, and particularly the chief boyar, behaved toward me and my young brother, Yuri; how they kept us in dire poverty and prevented us from eating our fill; how Shuisky compelled me,

Yelena Glinskaya and her young son Ivan (top left) inspect newly minted coins. During her regency for Ivan, Yelena relied on the counsel of her lover, Prince Ivan Telepnev-Obolensky. When she died in 1538, young Ivan was left to the mercy of the ruling boyars.

the tsar, to wear his son's old clothes. One day Shuisky called me in order to remonstrate with me; he was in my father's bedroom and, sitting on the bed with his foot on the pillow, he flouted me and adopted toward me, the tsar and sovereign, a contemptuous attitude."

When the occasion demanded, however, the Shuiskys would make good use of young Ivan. When a foreign ambassador had to be received, they would dress the boy in the full regalia of a grand prince and pretend to pay homage to him. But at other times, they deprived him of food and clothes and of those closest to him. When Ivan was eight, he lost his nurse, and three years later, the Shuiskys removed from his company a boyar named Fyodor Vorontsov, who had befriended the quiet boy.

Ivan was a serious and studious child. He was an avid reader and quickly mastered the literature available to him. He read works on world history, Greek history in particular, and he knew the stories of the great rulers — King Solomon and Alexander the Great, the emperors of Constantinople and the Turkish sultans, and the khans of the Mongol Golden Horde, who ruled still to the south and east of Russia. In addition, he became thoroughly acquainted with the Bible and Russian religious history and could recite from memory long biblical passages.

At the same time, however, Ivan already was showing signs of cruelty and an unbridled temper. These tendencies were anything but stifled by his teachers and advisers, who brought the boy to witness tortures and executions or encouraged him to throw cats and dogs from the high walls of the Kremlin (the fortified collection of palaces and churches from which Moscow's rulers governed) and then inspect the splattered remains on the ground. Ivan thus grew up absorbing images of pain and death.

Almost two years after Ivan's midnight scare by supporters of the Shuiskys, the precocious and turbulent youth, embittered by his rough treatment at the hands of Andrei Shuisky, decided to test his power. He ordered his servants to seize Shuisky and fling him into the kennels, where fierce hunting dogs were kept. The boyar was set upon and killed. His remains were gathered and disposed of in a pit where executed prisoners were buried.

The boyars and the people of Moscow soon came to realize the nature and strength of Ivan. It may have been from this time that the young prince was known as Ivan Groznyi (from *groza*, Russian for thunder). In English his name is usually translated as Ivan the Terrible but actually is more truly rendered as Ivan the Awe-Inspiring or the Dread. (Some scholars maintain that Ivan's epithet dates from his capture of Kazan. The name seems originally to have been a term of respect, an acknowledgment of Ivan's power.)

Although he clearly had become undisputed ruler of Moscow, Ivan continued to search for a way to make that vividly apparent to all his subjects. He spent a great deal of time studying, especially the Scriptures, and eventually came upon the idea of having himself crowned tsar (the Russian form of Caesar) in the manner of the Roman and Byzantine emperors. Ivan's idea was that by adopting that ancient title he would demonstrate to the still restless boyars that he, and he alone, ruled Moscow. To emphasize his connection to imperial Byzantium (his grandmother had been a Byzantine princess), Ivan formally adopted the Byzantine double-headed eagle on his coat of arms. There was no doubt, however, that he also meant to stress his preeminence in the Russian tradition. As a descendant of Rurik, traditionally the founder of "Rus" (Russia), Ivan would don the fur-trimmed crown of Monomakh, the symbol of legitimate Russian rulers. To add further credibility to the coronation, Ivan even sought to have his coronation sanctioned by the patriarch of Constantinople, still officially the head of the Orthodox church, to which Ivan and most of his subjects were devoted. Although Ivan accompanied his suggestion with handsome presents, his request was not granted by the time he was officially crowned Tsar and Autocrat of All Russia on January 16, 1547. Not until 1561 did the patriarch send a document

SOVFOTO

The double-headed eagle, a Byzantine symbol, signified Moscow's role as successor to the great empires of Rome and Byzantium. Ivan used the symbol on his coat of arms.

The crown of Monomakh was the traditional symbol of Russian rulers. By donning the crown, which is made of gold and edged with sable fur, Ivan wished to show his legitimacy as a descendant of Rurik, the founder of ancient Russia.

saying: "I certify by this investiture the power of the Tsar implies sovereignty by divine right, which is answerable neither to the people nor to the monastic orders."

After the ceremony that winter day in 1547, the 16-year-old Ivan went in procession through the Kremlin gates to a dais in Red Square to address his subjects. Red Square — *Krasnaya Ploshchad* in Russian — is the main square beside the Kremlin. It did not acquire its present name, which was originally translated as "beautiful" (*krasnaya* can mean both red and beautiful) until the 17th century. In Ivan's time, the square was called *pozharnaya ploshchad*, from the Russian word for fire, which continually threatened the wooden structures there, or simply "the Square."

Like so many of Ivan's speeches and writings, his coronation address was introspective. It dealt with his personal feelings but — and this was especially surprising, given the age of the tsar — it carried powerful threats for those who did not obey him. "I lost my parents too early," he said. "The boyars took no thought for me, for they meant to govern themselves. In my name they seized offices; and they enriched themselves by their injustices and oppressed the people. . . . You boyars did as you liked, foul rebels and unjust judges that you were! What answer can you give me today? What tears have you not wrung from others, what blood have you not shed? I am guiltless of that blood. But as for you, a terrible judgment of Heaven awaits you!"

The land over which the new tsar ruled was surrounded by enemies and inhabited by impoverished peasants and boyars seeking to increase their own power. To the west, the powerful Catholic states of Poland and Lithuania threatened to overrun Russian territory. To the east, the warlike Kazan Tatars posed a serious threat to Russian settlements. In the south, Tatars in the Crimea, on the Black Sea, and Astrakhan, on the Caspian Sea, with the active support of the Turks in Constantinople, were constantly raiding Russian territory and frequently attacked Moscow itself.

COLLECTION VIOLLET

The coronation of Ivan in 1547. With the formal adoption of the title of tsar, (derived from "Caesar," used by the Byzantine emperors), Ivan made clear his intention to consolidate power in his own person.

It is hard to imagine the terror that these Tatar invasions must have struck in the Russian people. For over two centuries Russia had been subject to the brutalities of rule by the Tatar Golden Horde, the Mongol horsemen from the east, who had first invaded Russia in the mid-13th century. Russia had won a measure of relief only after the Battle of Kulikovo in 1380, when the Muscovite Dmitri Donskoi defeated the Tatars. In 1480 Ivan's grandfather Ivan III (the Great) had broken the stranglehold the Golden Horde kept on Russia, but the Tatars maintained strong kingdoms, called khanates, in Kazan, Astrakhan, and the Crimea.

According to contemporary accounts, each spring the Tatars would ride north out of their stronghold in the Crimean Peninsula to raid Russian towns and villages, burning and looting without mercy. One of their chief aims was to capture children to be sold in the slave markets of Asia, where the fair, blue-

In assuming the title of Tsar . . . [Ivan] was adorning the Russian monarchy with the title that announced his claim to the leadership of all true Christians and at the same time to political headship of "the universe."
—MELVIN C. WREN
American historian

eyed Russians brought very high prices. The children's parents were usually killed immediately, but the youngsters were bundled into special nets that hung from the Tatar saddles, their hands and feet bound with thongs. Trussed up this way, they were carried many miles — often hundreds of miles — across the steppes (the south Russian plains) back to the Crimea. There, the Tatars gathered in a huge camp. Any children who were sick or injured were slaughtered out of hand. The rest — often tens of thousands in a single year—went into slavery.

Moscow's dominance of Russia was not completely accepted by other Russian cities, such as Novgorod and Pskov (to the northwest), which had formerly enjoyed an autonomy denied them now. Ivan's predecessors periodically had tried to subjugate the rival cities, but opposition to Moscow persisted and occasionally flared up. These rivalries were further complicated by the role of the Russian

Old Moscow in the 16th century, with a view of the Kremlin walls. In June 1547 a devastating fire destroyed much of the city. After superstitious peasants blamed Ivan's uncle for the blaze and killed him, Ivan ordered the summary execution of the instigators.

Orthodox church. As with the secular powers, there was rivalry between the church leaders of Moscow, Novgorod, and Pskov as well as periodic antagonism between the ecclesiastical leaders and the tsar, the secular ruler. Thus the relationship between the metropolitan of Moscow and the ruler often was tied to political events. Ivan especially seemed to maintain throughout his life an ambivalent relationship with the church leaders. He alternated between respect for their position and rage against their interference in his affairs.

Ivan was determined to increase Moscow's influence, and for a young man he was unusually farsighted in determining what should be done to achieve this end. For example, soon after his installation as tsar, he decided—and the decision does seem to have been his — that it was necessary for him to marry quickly and wisely.

This was no simple matter because the Russian customs involved in the ruler's marriage were extremely complicated. The first requirement was the holding of a gathering called a *smotriny*, in which eligible girls were gathered from all over the country. They were examined by priests for their fitness and Christian virtues and by doctors and women relatives of the tsar to make sure they were virgins. In Ivan's case, the smotriny was superintended by his grandmother, Princess Anna Glinskaya. It was the most elaborate such ceremony held up to that date and attracted so many young women that the terem of the Kremlin had to be enlarged considerably. To augment the splendor of the occasion, new windows of Venetian glass, a great rarity in Russia, where most windows were still covered with hides scraped thin, were installed in the Kremlin. In addition, a grand new church was built within the walls of the Kremlin.

Ivan's choice as his bride was the beautiful Anastasia Romanova, a child of a well-known Moscow family in service to the tsar. The Romanov family in later centuries would play the leading role in the rise and fall of tsarist Russia. The royal marriage was celebrated on February 3, 1547, and by all accounts was serene. Anastasia possessed the rare ability of being able to calm her turbulent husband, and he seems to have been genuinely in love with her.

But troubles continued to plague Ivan. Four months after his marriage a great fire swept through Moscow, destroying three-quarters of the city and damaging parts of the Kremlin itself, including the great bell tower erected by Ivan I. The inferno had started in the section of Moscow called the Arbat, where there were many shops and taverns. Ivan removed himself and his family to the

archevêque
en habit ordinaire
au chœurs

A Russian Orthodox archbishop. Ivan both feared and hated the clergy. Although capable of frightful barbarity, Ivan had a deeply ingrained religious sense that often led him to donate money to the church to pray for the people he killed.

safety of the nearby Sparrow Hills, where he watched the rapid progress of the blaze. Many of the common people, however, had great difficulty getting out of the way of the flames and perished in their attempts to flee. Metropolitan Makary, Russia's most powerful religious leader, was nearly trapped in his home inside the Kremlin. He finally escaped by being lowered by rope over the Kremlin walls to the bank of the Moscow River below. Only a change of wind prevented even worse disaster. Such events were not rare in Moscow, where almost all of the buildings except some churches and palaces were contructed of wood. If a fire started in one building it was difficult to prevent it from spreading to another. It is estimated that fires nearly destroyed the city every 20 years. On this occasion, the family of the murdered Andrei Shuisky spread rumors that the fire had been caused by the practice of black magic by the Glinsky family. Among the superstitious peasants who made up most of Moscow's population, such tales were eagerly believed and spread as quickly as fire itself.

A crowd of several thousand people milled in front of the Kremlin gates and demanded the death of Ivan's uncle Yuri Glinsky and his grandmother Anna Glinskaya for the terrible calamity brought upon the city. It did not take the mob long to break through the gates, and as the angry throng pursued Prince Yuri, he fled to what he thought was the sanctuary of the Uspensky Cathedral. His pursuers caught up with him there and murdered him on the altar steps, then set about to loot the cathedrals and homes in the Kremlin. When a menacing crowd arrived at Ivan's residence on the Sparrow Hills, the young tsar ordered his soldiers to charge the rioters. Some of those held responsible for instigating the uprising were hanged on a specially erected gallows in Red Square. Ivan himself watched the executions. As he left, he handed a purse containing a large sum of money to Metropolitan Philip of Moscow with orders that every year, on the anniversary of the riot, the cleric should pray for the souls of the hanged men.

Die Bildnus Iwan
Wasilewicz des Kyser
Gros fürsten in Reussen
oder Moschkaw

So war erwelt recht in der Figur
Dye warhafftig Kontrafaitur
Sein weissen vnd mit farb ergbildt
Sein Kleydung, Bärten vnd Gestalt

Der Grosfürst er Iwan dz ich
Iwan Wasilawicz
Der Moschkaw erwelt vnd genant
Der ytzt mit getwaltiger Hand
Auss Nowgarten vnder Hauptstett
Hat weiberg Herr gesetzt ptzt
Wider Polacko vnuerthan
Die machtigen Künig zu Polan

Gedruckt zu Nürmberg durch
Hans Weygel Form
schneyder

2

The Good Years

Despite the violence of such episodes as the Red Square executions, the early years of Ivan's reign were a generally prosperous and benign time for the Russian people. For this reason, his rule is often described as having two parts: the good years immediately after he became tsar and the terrible time that followed Tsarina Anastasia's death in 1560. True, there were many executions and evil deeds carried out in the first part of his reign, but young Ivan was in many ways no harsher than other rulers of the time: King Henry VIII of England, Catherine de Médici of France, Sultan Suleiman the Magnificent of the Ottoman Empire, and King Philip II of Spain.

In Ivan's first years as tsar, he gathered around him skillful advisers, a kind of cabinet to which he gave the name of the Chosen Council. Most prominent in this council were a priest, Father Sylvester, who had been introduced to Ivan by Tsarina Anastasia and was the court chaplain, and Aleksei Adashev, who had entered the tsar's service as a court clerk. Metropolitan Makary was also a member. Father Sylvester was best known as the author of a set of ethical and religious rules, called the *Domostroy*, which Russian families would be taught for many years to come. Ivan's relationship with the

> *I think no prince in Christendom is more feared of his own than he is, nor better loved.*
> —ANTHONY JENKINSON
> British visitor, on Ivan in 1557

Despite his fearsome reputation, Ivan the Terrible's first years as tsar were marked by prudent governmental policies, attempts at modernization, and a willingness to heed his advisers.

Seen in the context of the harsh world of the 16th century, Ivan's early reign was no crueler than those of many other rulers of the day, such as Suleiman the Magnificent (pictured here), sultan of the Ottoman Empire (now Turkey).

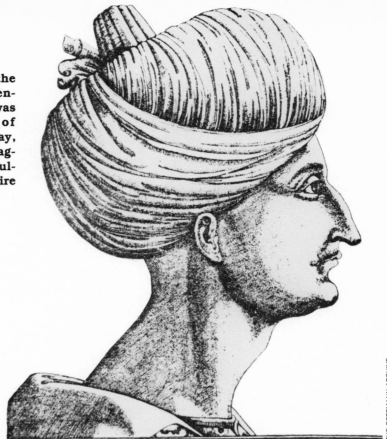

council was unusually cordial; he not only followed its advice in most matters, he even accepted criticism when its members thought he was acting mistakenly.

In some ways Ivan's rule during the period was a foretaste of that of Peter the Great, who was tsar from 1682 to 1725 and was responsible for westernizing Russia. For example, in 1547 Ivan dispatched a special envoy to western Europe to recruit scholars and skilled tradesmen to teach Russians more modern ways of doing things. As it turned out, only a few of those recruited reached Moscow. Many of them were prevented from doing so by European rulers, especially the Germans and Lithuanians, who wanted to keep Russia as backward as possible, particularly as far as military affairs were concerned.

The council urged that Ivan try to bring some semblance of order to Russia's domestic affairs.

With this in mind, in 1550 Ivan summoned a great assembly of delegates, a *Zemsky Sobor* (assembly of the land), to the Kremlin. There was a precedent for such a gathering; Ivan's grandfather, Ivan the Great, had called one in the late 15th century, before his invasion of Novgorod. But the 1550 Zemsky Sobor was to be much broader, including not just boyars and high-ranking clergy but representatives of all classes. Ivan himself spoke eloquently to the assembly and told the delegates that he had called them together to uncover the abuses in the land and to discuss means of removing them.

One result was that petitions from Ivan's subjects began to pour into the Kremlin in such numbers that Ivan instructed Adashev to set up a special office, the *prikaz*, to receive them. These petitions complained of murders, robberies, and other crimes that local governors had failed to prevent or punish or had even committed themselves. In response, Ivan removed some governors. To replace them he

In his desire for contact with the West, Ivan resembles Tsar Peter the Great, who in the early 18th century "westernized" Russia by importing craftsmen and military experts from Europe. Peter (foreground) is shown here consulting with Dutch naval experts.

Ivan III, known as Ivan the Great, was Ivan the Terrible's grandfather. He began the work of building Muscovite authority in the 15th century, laying the foundation for the Russian empire.

authorized the election of special judicial bodies whose responsibility was to deal with any criminals caught in their areas. These judiciaries had the power to condemn to death and execute criminals. Ivan also ordered a revision of the *Sudebnik*, the law code initiated by his grandfather. He also had Adashev overhaul the way in which judges were appointed, finding better men to preside over the courts.

Despite these enlightened reforms, police and judicial affairs remained inordinately backward. Punishments were often cruel and even sadistic. Torture was commonly used to extract confessions. The knout, a whip with iron-hard knots on its thongs, was used against those who committed even minor crimes. Sometimes it was used to lash prisoners to death.

For two years, the tsar was deeply concerned with trying to improve life for the average Russian and bringing order to the business of the state. As part of this drive, in 1551, Ivan paid special attention to reforming the affairs of the Orthodox church, in

It was always found . . . that the man who was in the right and had sworn an oath was not in the right if the other party had more money.
—German visitor to Ivan's court, on corruption in the Muscovite government

A 17th-century view of Novgorod. Ivan the Great had called together a general assembly in the late 15th century to approve his invasion of the city. Using his grandfather's precedent, Ivan the Terrible called together a *Zemsky Sobor* (assembly of the land) in 1550 to discuss war against the Tatars.

WELIKI NOVOGORD ODER GROS NAVGARD

what became known as the *Stoglav*, or Council of a Hundred Chapters. When the council's decisions were finally read to the public in the Uspensky Cathedral in the Kremlin, important changes were revealed. The church, for example, lost the right to acquire more land without the tsar's specific permission. As a forum for settling administrative disputes within the church, each 100 priests were to elect an elder whose task it was to call special meetings that would decide on solutions. Ivan intended these elders to wield authority in more than just church matters, however. In another speech before the Zemsky Sobor, he said, "From now on it will be the custom of our country and a tradition for our children to consult the elders every time events make it necessary to do so."

In 1552 Ivan further increased the power of local populations by giving them greater control over the collection of taxes. When a community promised a fixed sum in taxes to the state treasury, it could elect its own local officials to collect the money rather than being subject to an appointed governor. In addition, in those areas where governors still held power, the people were allowed to elect assessors to keep a watch on how the governors performed. These assessors even had the power to impeach appointed officials if necessary.

All the measures Ivan took to increase the authority of local officials and check arbitrary judicial and clerical decisions reflected the tsar's desire to strip as much power as he could from the boyars. Though Ivan was very religious and keenly felt his duty was to improve the lot of his subjects, his actions often pointed to the same political goal: the destruction of the boyar class as a political entity and the concomitant centralization of power in the hands of the tsar.

Ivan was also absorbed at this time with military matters. He was responsible for the formation of new companies of artillerymen and engineers and also created the Russian army's first permanent units of infantrymen armed with muskets. These musketeers, the nucleus of the Russian army, were

A lieutenant colonel of the *streltsy*, the corps of musketeers created by Ivan to modernize the Russian army. Ivan's efforts to upgrade the Russian military also included the formation of artillery and engineering companies.

given the name *streltsy* — literally, "archers" — and in future years were to play a pivotal role in Russian history. They served as full-time soldiers but were also given substantial commercial concessions, which they guarded jealously. At the time of their formation, however, they were merely part of Ivan's drive to modernize Moscow.

All these changes were important, but perhaps the most significant move by the Zemsky Sobor was taken just before it finished its sessions. It "instructed" the tsar to take action to liberate that part of Russia still under threat from raids by the Kazan Tatars.

3

Victory in Kazan

There were many reasons why the Zemsky Sobor urged an attack on Kazan. There was a political one — a need to free Russian territory from control of the Tatars. There was a religious reason — the Tatars were Muslims, the Russians were Christian. There were trade reasons as well.

Since time immemorial, trade in Russia had followed the region's great rivers — the Dnieper, the Moscow, the Don, and of course the Volga. But the Volga, on which Kazan was strategically situated, was firmly in the hands of the Tatars, which meant that Russian trade was cut off from access to Asia, the source of so many desirable goods such as spices and silk. Matters were made worse because trade with Europe was largely prevented by the hostile presence of Poland and Lithuania.

Ivan had been given an opportune time to attack Kazan. The great Volga city had been founded about 1400 as the capital of a splinter group of the Golden Horde. It was ruled by a khan who nominally owed allegiance to the Great Khan (who remained in Asia) but was largely independent. In the middle of the 16th century, a dispute arose over who should be khan in Kazan. At one stage of the dispute, a nominee friendly to Moscow had been installed, but the people of Kazan sought to depose him and replace

[I am determined to free Muscovy] from the ferocity of these external enemies with whom there can be neither peace nor rest.
—IVAN THE TERRIBLE
on the Tatars

While still in his early twenties, Ivan saw the opportunity to use bold military action to expand his empire by exploiting internal divisions among the Tatars, the descendants of the Mongol horsemen who had invaded Russia in the mid-13th century.

NOVOSTI PRESS AGENCY

The Tatars dominated large areas of southern Russia and Siberia when Ivan the Terrible moved against them in 1552. Once a nomadic people, the Tatars had become mostly settled agriculturists by the 16th century but still made forays into Russia for slaves.

him with a prince from Astrakhan, the khanate on the Caspian Sea. Amid the upheaval caused by these changes, Ivan assembled an expedition of 100,000 men and 150 cannon and after many solemn religious ceremonies set out for the Volga in June 1552. The procession included one of Moscow's most sacred religious relics, the Cross of Dmitri Donskoi. Prince Dmitri had been the victor over the Tatars at the Battle of Kulikovo nearly two centuries earlier.

The great dangers of the expedition were quickly made clear. Sensing that Ivan's departure left the way to Moscow open, the Crimean Tatars immediately attacked northward. They penetrated as far north as the city of Tula, a key outpost south of Moscow. Ivan was almost diverted from his march on Kazan by the threat, but after a short siege of Tula, which held firm, the Crimean Tatars returned to the south.

Finally Ivan's troops reached the Volga. New setbacks faced them there. Boats and supplies sank trying to cross the mighty river. The enemy garrison of 30,000 men was well protected behind the walls of the great Tatar fortress and ignored repeated demands that they surrender. A high tower built by the Russians to give them a view over the walls was almost captured by a Tatar raiding party. Roving bands of Tatar guerrillas harassed Ivan's rearguard troops at every opportunity.

Then the Russians cut off the fortress's water supply. After several weeks of great hardship among the defenders, in October 1552 Ivan gave the order to storm Kazan. To facilitate entry to the city, Ivan's troops dug a tunnel under the wall and placed a great quantity of gunpowder there. When it was exploded, a great section of the wall collapsed and the Russian soldiers surged into Kazan. Among the first through the breached wall was 24-year-old Prince Andrei Kurbsky. He would be a hero of that day's bloody struggle, but eventually he would become a bitter enemy of the tsar.

Prince Dmitri Donskoi of Moscow leads his soldiers in prayer before the decisive battle against the Tatars at Kulikovo in 1380. Dmitri's victory was the first major Russian defeat of the Tatar Golden Horde.

The economic aim underlying the campaign against the Kazan Tatars was to free Russian shipping and trade along the Volga River, which was severely constrained by the Tatar presence. In October of 1552 Ivan's siege of Kazan resulted in a resounding victory.

He saw himself as another Joshua or another Gideon, leading his people to the promised land, smiting the enemy with terrible blows.

—ROBERT PAYNE and NIKITA ROMANOFF historians, on Ivan's march to Kazan

The Tatars fought to the end. Even the grand mullah, the Tatar religious leader, died trying to defend the city's mosque from the invaders. In one last, futile gesture 6,000 Tatars burst out of the city, leaving their armor behind, and engaged the Russians in hand-to-hand fighting. The odds were overwhelmingly against them, and most of them perished. Kazan itself was leveled by fire.

Ivan returned to Moscow in triumph. A great religious service of thanksgiving was held in the Kremlin, at which Ivan and Metropolitan Philip made fiery patriotic speeches. Three new towers were erected to commemorate the victory. Ivan ordered the construction, just outside the Kremlin walls, of a new cathedral that would be more spectacular than any inside the citadel. To supervise the construction, two Russian architects came from nearby Pskov, and the cathedral, with its soaring, gloriously colored onion domes and its interior maze of interlocking chapels, is unmistakably Russian in design.

The Cathedral of St. Basil the Blessed, completed in 1560, is one of the world's great landmarks. St. Basil's was originally called the Cathedral of the Intercession of the Virgin, later adopting its present name from a holy beggar of Moscow. The church, constructed of wood, boasts a series of octagonal towers, eight cupolas, each of a different design, and eleven separate steeples. The cathedral's striking exterior colors, which include blue, gold, red, green, and purple, offer a sharp contrast to the medieval, somber interior with its low doors, dark, winding passages, and narrow, steep stairs. Legends about its origin persist, including the dubious story that when the work was done Ivan ordered the architect to be blinded so that he could never duplicate his Red Square masterpiece.

Although the entire khanate would not be secured by the Russians for another five years, the capture of Kazan opened the way for further Russian penetration of the Ural Mountains and eastward into the vast land of Siberia. To further consolidate Moscow's hold over its eastern frontier, in 1556 Prince Kurbsky led an army in an attack on Astrakhan,

THE BETTMANN ARCHIVE

The Cathedral of St. Basil the Blessed (completed in 1560) was constructed in honor of Ivan's victory at Kazan. Ivan ordered the spectacular cathedral built just outside the Kremlin walls.

Tatars on the march. After the fall of Kazan, the Tatars of Astrakhan and the Crimea continued to raid Russian territory. The Russians captured Astrakhan in 1556, but their campaign to defeat the Crimean Tatars was halted by the intercession of the powerful Ottoman Turks.

where the Volga (the sacred Ityl to the Tatars) emptied into the Caspian Sea. Kurbsky was soon victorious, and the great lifeline of Russia, "Mother Volga," was securely in Russian hands. Ivan annexed Astrakhan that same year.

Now Moscow was in direct contact with the heart of Asia. It was therefore natural that before long there arrived in the Russian capital a delegation from the shah of Persia with a present for Ivan. It was a huge elephant, and it was said to have been trained to bow in homage before the tsar. People came from all over Moscow and the surrounding area to see this strange creature. Eventually Ivan himself, accompanied by a large retinue of officials, came to see it. He ordered it to bow before him, but the animal stubbornly refused. Ivan grew angry. "Cut it to pieces," he shouted. Within minutes the animal lay hacked to death by the lances and axes of Ivan's soldiers.

Now only the Crimean Tatars threatened southern Russia. Kurbsky and Adashev supported the idea of a campaign to subdue the Crimean Tatars, although Ivan himself seems to have been opposed to the idea. The tsar feared that the long march across the hot, dry Ukrainian steppes was too dangerous. The tsar was also wary of antagonizing the powerful Ottoman Turks, just to the south of the Crimea.

The tsar yielded, however, and Kurbsky led his men south, where they first intercepted and defeated a Tatar slaving expedition returning to the Crimea from a raid into Russia. The horrified Russians freed 25,000 captive countrymen, of whom about 15,000 were children.

Kurbsky then attacked the narrow Perekop Isthmus, the entrance to the Crimea. Such was the force of the Russian attack that the Tatars retreated about 40 miles into the Crimea. This defeat, however, alarmed the Turkish sultan, of whom the Tatars were nominal subjects, and he quickly sent a fleet to land troops to support them. Afraid of being cut off, Kurbsky halted his campaign, but not before he set fire to the Tatar capital. His troops carried back to Moscow with them a gift for the tsar — a magnificent block of pink Carrara marble, which was used to make a column for the Grand Palace in the Kremlin.

This was a time of relative prosperity and progress in Ivan's realm. He eagerly sought to modernize Russian society; it was at this time, for example, that he arranged to have Russia's first printing works established in Moscow. Metropolitan Makary set up the press in 1553, which, after a hesitant start, produced the first printed book in the Russian language, a life of St. Basil. (The press was soon closed because the common people regarded it as a source of foreign witchcraft, and it did not reopen again until 1568.) Other enterprises were also promoted, among them a huge new saltworks, near the Ural Mountains, owned by the Stroganov family, that was later to be highly important in the development of Siberia.

The events to the east and the south had been of great importance to Moscow, but at about the same time Ivan was engaged in another opening, this time to the west — to England in particular. Ivan wanted to establish a port on the Baltic Sea to connect Moscow to Europe. This desire, however, would bring the tsar into conflict with his powerful western neighbors and draw him into the longest war of his reign.

SOVFOTO

In 1553 Ivan appointed Ivan Fyodorov, shown here, to run Russia's first printing press. This early effort at westernization was short-lived, however, because the people of Moscow thought the press was a source of foreign witchcraft.

4

The Elusive Window to the West

Ivan was well aware of the technical and artistic advantages that Moscow could obtain through greater trade and contact with the nations of western Europe. By the same token, Moscow's neighbors, particularly Poland, Sweden, and the states established by the German crusading orders along the Baltic Sea, knew that it was in their interests to prevent Ivan from achieving those contacts.

Some time later, a Polish king would write to England's Queen Elizabeth I, urging her not to traffic with the Russians. This trade, the Polish ruler complained, allowed "The Muscovite, enemy to all liberty under the heavens, daily to grow mightier by the increase of . . . not only wares but also weapons heretofore unknown to him and artificers and arts; . . . by means whereof he makes himself strong to vanquish all others."

The English did not follow the Polish advice. In May 1553, an English company of "merchant adventurers" dedicated to the exploration of foreign lands, under the leadership of the famous explorer

He sets his whole delight upon two things: first, to serve God . . . and the second, how to subdue and conquer his enemies.
—British traveler, on Ivan in the 1550s

Ivan's desire to cement an alliance with the West, particularly with England, grew out of the threat he faced from Poland, Lithuania, and Sweden. These neighboring countries sought to keep Russia isolated and weak and opposed Ivan's plans to obtain a port on the Baltic Sea.

The English explorer Sebastian Cabot, famous for his expeditions to the New World, outfitted a voyage to seek new routes to China and India in 1553. The English landed in Russia instead and obtained lucrative trade concessions from Ivan, which angered Moscow's powerful merchants.

Sebastian Cabot, sent three ships, commanded by Sir Hugh Willoughby and Richard Chancellor, to seek a new route to China and India, northeastward through the Arctic Ocean. Bad weather delayed their passage and winter closed in on them before Willoughby and two of the ships had a chance to prepare for it. The two ships were locked in the ice, and Willoughby and all his men perished. Chancellor, however, was more fortunate and in September managed to reach the White Sea and sail to what is now Arkhangelsk (Archangel), at the mouth of the Northern Dvina River. There, he came across some fishermen and learned that he was in Russia.

Chancellor was carrying a letter from King Edward VI of England offering friendship to and seeking trade with any rulers the explorers might meet, which he now took personally to Ivan in Moscow. Ivan gave him a warm welcome and in the next few years the English were granted lucrative trade

concessions in Russia, including the right to conduct trade without paying any taxes and to hire and dismiss their own workers. They also enjoyed various protections against seizure of their goods and arrest for debt. More significantly, Ivan appointed a special court official with jurisdiction over the English, and the tsar himself heard any case involving an Englishman breaking Russian law. The merchants in Moscow were bitterly unhappy about the special privileges granted the English, and Ivan realized how heavy a price he was paying for English goodwill, but he hoped to secure England as a possible future ally against Poland and Lithuania.

To cement the new alliance, a Russian ambassador, Osip Nepea, was sent to London, which he reached in February 1557 only after a perilous voyage in which the ship carrying him was wrecked off the coast of Scotland, where Chancellor drowned in a heroic effort to save the Russian envoy's life. The Russian was treated sumptuously in London, however, and returned home with several English experts in mining and medicine under contract.

However, what Ivan really wanted from the English was modern arms and instruction from English experts in handling them. London would receive protests from states as far apart as Sweden (which had an eye on Baltic Sea territory for itself)

Russian diplomacy began with Ivan's efforts to open trade and political ties to the West. Shown here are Russia's ambassadors to the German court of Maximilian II, emperor of the Holy Roman Empire.

and Venice about reported sales of arms to the Russians, but the lure of the inexhaustible supply of rich Russian furs and the possibility of using Russian land routes to tap Asian trade seems to have persuaded the British to comply with some of his requests for munitions.

In 1553 Ivan had fallen critically ill. Once again the ancient divisions in his kingdom came to the fore. He wanted the boyars to swear that if he died they would acknowledge his infant son, Dmitri, as the new tsar. But this plan for succession was opposed by some of the boyars, especially Ivan's cousin Prince Vladimir of Staritsa, who wanted the throne for himself. Behind their opposition was the fear that should Ivan die while his son was still a baby, the Romanov family — the child's maternal relatives, who would assume the regency for a minor — would have too much power. Even Father Sylvester and Adashev, Ivan's closest advisers, took Vladimir's side. Ivan insisted, however, and the fearful boyars, including Prince Vladimir, complied. But opposition to his wishes had been revealed, and the deep-seated distrust of the boyar class ingrained in Ivan from his youth led the tsar to imagine widespread disloyalty on the part of his boyars. The incident was to have great repercussions later in the violent final chapters of Ivan's reign.

Ivan recovered from his illness and regained his interest in seeking greater and more direct access to the rest of Europe. In this desire he was following the policy of Ivan the Great and Vasili III, who had both sought to increase Moscow's territory on the eastern rim of the Baltic. He faced the same obstacles. In 1558, after some debate over whether it might be wiser to finally drive the Tatars from the Crimea first, Ivan launched a new Russian drive toward the Baltic.

Over the past century, Moscow had periodically forced its way onto the shores of the Baltic Sea, but every time the Russians had been driven back. The latest reverses had occurred in the reign of Ivan's father, and Ivan meant now to recover the lost territory.

The immediate target was Livonia, comprising parts of what are now the Soviet Republics of Estonia and Latvia. At the time it was ruled by the Livonian Order, one of the German orders of crusading knights, which had originally established a settlement along the Baltic Sea coast in the 13th century. The territory held by the orders became part of the important trading system, controlled by the Germans, between eastern and western Europe. By Ivan's time, the Livonian land was divided among members of the order, who were unable or unwilling to present a united front in the face of Muscovite aggression. They perhaps expected aid from the Holy Roman Empire (a loosely structured state composed primarily of German principalities, Austria, and Bohemia), to which Livonia technically belonged, but the empire was far more concerned with the Ottoman threat from the south than with a distant Baltic squabble.

Ivan knew that Livonia was a weak state, and although his closest advisers, Father Sylvester and Adashev, apparently opposed the campaign, he rushed it ahead as fast as he could. Ivan's initial thrust in 1558 was successful. His troops quickly conquered the important cities of Neuhaus, Narva, and Dorpat. The success at Dorpat, or Yuriev, as it was known in Russian, was especially gratifying. Now called Tartu, it had been regarded as a Russian city since its founding five centuries earlier by Prince Yaroslav the Wise of Kiev. At Narva a number of merchant ships fell into the Russians' hands and were soon converted into a war fleet, the first substantial Russian navy on the Baltic, although the ships were officered by foreigners.

The success of Ivan's forces led to the disbanding of the Livonian Order in 1561, but it also aroused the hostility of Sweden, Poland, and Lithuania, all of which had ambitions to control the eastern part of the Baltic.

Realizing that his forces were no match for Ivan's, the last grand master of the Livonians, Gotthard Kettler, made a deal with Poland, in which he received a hereditary duchy in return for service to

SOVFOTO

The Livonian city of Dorpat (now Tartu) was founded by Prince Yaroslav the Wise, the 11th-century ruler of Kiev. The city's Russian origins and its strategic and commercial importance made it an attractive objective of Ivan's 1558 invasion of the Baltic region.

Sigismund II Augustus, king of Poland and grand duke of Lithuania. Poland and Lithuania realized the advantage of joining forces in the face of Muscovite aggression and launched a combined offensive against Ivan in 1563. Once again the tide seemed to flow in Ivan's favor. The new artillery regiments were successful in capturing the city of Polotsk on the Dvina River, giving the Russians an open line to the major city of Riga. The Poles won some minor engagements but soon sought to make peace. The war in the west, however, would drag on for years. Of more immediate importance was Ivan's personal life and the trauma that caused a dramatic change in the tsar.

In 1560 Ivan received the worst blow of his life when his beloved young wife died. Anastasia's life had not been an easy one. She had watched as her gravely ill husband tried to wrangle promises from his reluctant boyars and advisers. She had been forced to cope with her own and Ivan's grief at the death of their son and heir, Dmitri, in 1553, while on a pilgrimage to visit the great cities and the holy places throughout Russia. The following year, however, had brought renewed joy when Tsarevich Ivan was born. In 1558 Anastasia bore another son, Fyodor, but the child was sickly.

In the fall of 1559 Ivan and Anastasia traveled to the monastery at Mozhaisk, where the tsarina fell

Sigismund II Augustus, king of Poland and grand duke of Lithuania. The Polish king absorbed the territory of Livonia when the ruling German crusading order crumbled before the Russian forces.

ill. The doctors were unable to diagnose or treat her sickness, and the following July she suffered a second attack. Another serious fire had broken out in the Arbat, again threatening to engulf the city and causing new anxiety for the tsar and his ailing wife. In desperation Ivan moved Anastasia to Kolomenskoye, just outside of Moscow. But Anastasia never recovered; she died on August 7. Ivan in his grief wept uncontrollably, and at the funeral the tsar's aides had to support him to prevent his falling to the ground.

Ivan became convinced that Anastasia had been poisoned by the boyars, who were jealous of the influence of the Romanov family. The circumstances surrounding Anastasia's death have been woven into numerous legends, none of them provable. One version has her quarreling violently on her sickbed with Adashev over favors sought by her family, falling into an apoplectic fit, and dying some hours later. Whether there was any truth to it or not, Ivan certainly came to blame Adashev for his loss. When Adashev tried to console him, the tsar shouted: "May all the fiends possess you! I want no more of you, you murderer!" He burned hundreds of votive candles in her memory and for a considerable period was inconsolable. Ivan tried to shut out all that reminded him of his past and even packed off his two young sons to live in a special palace apart from him.

Within a short time of his beloved Anastasia's death, Ivan began talks with the Poles about a possible marriage to a Polish princess. The idea of linking the royal families of Poland and Moscow was politically attractive. The proposals were unsuccessful, however, and Ivan, seeking an ally in the still vulnerable south, married the daughter of a prince from the Caucasus. She was a Muslim, but before her marriage she was baptized a Christian and took the Christian name Maria Temriukovna. Although Ivan seemed to have recovered from Anastasia's death enough to make a politically advantageous marriage, no one appeared to understand the extent of his intense emotional distress.

SOVFOTO

The 12th-century Virgin of Vladimir icon. Ivan and his beloved wife, Anastasia, made many pilgrimages to Russian monasteries and holy sites. In 1559, in the monastery at Mozhaisk, Anastasia contracted the illness that killed her the following year.

IOVAN
BASILLI
GRᾱ DVCA
DI MOSCOVIA
stampato nouamente

5

Breaking with the Past

Ivan now began a turbulent period in his life in which he quarreled with all those who had befriended and supported him in the past. He was 30 years old, and it had been more than 13 years since he had been crowned tsar. During that time, Anastasia had been one of the few able to cope with and calm the violent mood swings of her husband.

In addition to his personal reasons, Ivan had state matters over which to quarrel with his advisers. Adashev and Sylvester had sided with a faction of the Moscow boyars who had opposed the war against Livonia. Sylvester, in particular, had wanted to postpone the Livonian campaign until the Crimean Tatars had first been overcome. The Tatars continued to be a threat, and every spring their raids into Russia carried off more booty and slaves. On occasion they still penetrated as far north as Moscow itself. The priest, seemingly oblivious to Ivan's desires, saw the conquest of the Muslim Tatars as almost a holy mission, the religious duty of the tsar.

The boyars opposed Ivan's Livonian War on more practical grounds. They selfishly did not want to spend their money or the lives of their sons and servants for a cause in which they had little belief

After the death of Anastasia the story of Ivan is one of unrelieved tragedy. . . . His character seemed to change overnight.
—ROBERT PAYNE and NIKITA ROMANOFF historians

Devastated by the loss of Anastasia in 1560, Ivan suddenly turned against his advisers. When members of the nobility and Chosen Council objected to his military campaign in Livonia, the tsar sought to silence their criticism by exile, imprisonment, and execution.

or of which they had little understanding. If anything, they resented the foreigners and the new ideas that Ivan had welcomed, and for that reason they wanted no part of further opening up a door to the West by way of the Baltic.

But Ivan would not brook any opposition. He was tired, he said, "of being told how long to sleep and how to dress." He said he was expected "to say nothing to his advisers but to let them say anything" to him. "If I try to object," he wrote, "they shout at me that my soul is lost." Ivan was especially bitter at what he saw as Adashev's "treachery." After all, the tsar said, he had taken Adashev, who had been born

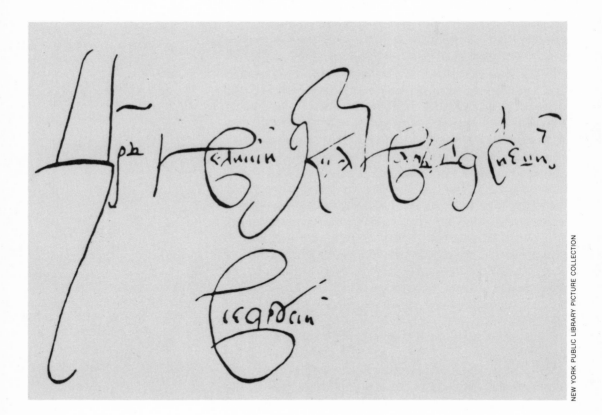

Ivan's signature, which reads: "Tsar and Grand Prince Ivan Vasilievich of all Russia." It is believed that Ivan did not actually sign any documents himself but rather had his chief secretary sign them for him.

poor and of low rank, "from the manure pile and placed him together with the nobles, hoping for faithful service from him. What honors and riches did I not heap upon him — not only on him, but on his family? Yet what true service did I get from him?"

Sylvester and Adashev were the first victims of Ivan's wrath. Ivan had been angered by their reluctance to support his Livonian campaign and their interference in his policies, and he turned on them completely after Anastasia's death. Sylvester was packed off to the Solovetsky Monastery in the remote north, on an island in the White Sea, where he remained for the rest of his life. Adashev, who had been appointed to lead troops in Livonia, was stripped of his command and arrested in Dorpat. He languished in prison for two months before he died, perhaps killed on Ivan's orders.

The rule of the Chosen Council had ended. All around him Ivan saw disloyalty and treason. He feared that the boyars were supporting one another, plotting against their tsar. He turned on the members of the council as well as their friends and relatives, and he began executing those who criticized him. During the Livonian War, some boyars had been caught planning to flee to Lithuania, and after Ivan began his executions, several more boyars left Moscow, fearful of the tsar's suspicions. This only fueled Ivan's paranoia, and he ordered the executions of anyone he suspected of escaping to the enemy or plotting against him.

As if to confirm his worst fears, Ivan discovered that one of the boyars who had escaped to Lithuania was Prince Andrei Kurbsky. Formerly one of the tsar's closest associates, Kurbsky now deserted him to avoid the gruesome fate already befalling his fellow boyars in Moscow. Kurbsky had been in charge of the Russian forces in the still unresolved war in Livonia. He now switched his allegiance to Poland, from where he sent Ivan a series of letters, which, along with the tsar's replies, forms one of the strangest sets of correspondence in history. The exchange began in 1564 and continued over the next 15 years.

He argued that in attacking the boyars he was only defending the throne God had placed in his keeping. . . . In all this, Ivan was looking forward to the strong, centralized nation-state.
—MELVIN C. WREN
American historian

Ivan (center) receives an emissary from Prince Andrei
Kurbsky. Formerly a close associate of the tsar, Kurbsky
escaped to Lithuania to avoid his wrath and sent Ivan
letters criticising him for his abuse of power and ill treatment of the boyars.

Kurbsky actively plotted with Moscow's enemies to achieve the overthrow of the tsar, and Ivan would certainly have executed Kurbsky if he could have laid his hands on him. But the two men, both strong, highly intelligent, and ambitious for their causes, retained enough of their past relationship to try to change the other's attitude. The correspondence is important because it focuses on the central conflict of 16th-century Russia — the nature of the new absolutism in Moscow. Kurbsky, the spokesman for the old system of independent boyar rule, essentially accused the tsar of abusing his power in his ill-treatment of the nobles. Ivan in turn taunted his foe with the specter of a state languishing under the decentralizing rule of numerous boyars — unable to agree on any issue, fighting among themselves for more power — who would reduce the land to the anarchy the tsar had witnessed as a child.

Kurbsky, the hero of Kazan and the Crimea, complained that his long and victorious service had brought him only trouble: "I have achieved most glorious conquests to increase your renown. And this, not in one year, nor yet in two — but throughout many years have I toiled with much sweat and patience; . . . Still more, I was visited with wounds inflicted by barbarian bands in various battles and all my body is already inflicted with sores. But to you, O tsar, was all this as nought; rather do you show us your intolerable wrath and bitter hatred, and, furthermore, burning pyres."

For his part, Ivan accused Kurbsky and the other boyars of trying to usurp the tsar's powers and trying to treat him like a child. He said he had been forgiving but that the boyars had continued in their mistaken behavior. He wrote, "And to you, our boyars, and to all our people did I grant forgiveness for your misdeeds and ruled that henceforth all memory of them be obliterated; and so then did we begin to treat you all as good men. But you did not abandon your first cunning habit but returned again to your former ways and thus began to serve us with cunning counsel and false, and to do everything with scheming and not with innocence."

> *You have recompensed me with evil for good and for my love with implacable hatred. My blood, spilt like water for you, cries out against you to the lord.*
> —PRINCE ANDREI KURBSKY
> from a letter to Ivan

The quarrels between Ivan and the boyars worsened after the death of Metropolitan Makary in 1563. After Anastasia's death the aged cleric had been almost the only person capable of restraining Ivan during the worst of his tempests. Now he, too, was gone. In addition, Ivan's brother, Yuri, had died earlier that same year. Ivan seems to have grown very despondent. One chill morning in December 1564, Moscow awoke to find that a strange event had taken place in the Kremlin during the night.

Sleighs had been drawn up beside the tsar's palace. Into them servants had loaded all of Ivan's treasures — his gold, his icons, and his books. Bundled up against the cold of the winter, Ivan, his two young sons, and his new wife got into the sleighs and then drove off. No one knew where the tsar had gone. When the news of his disappearance spread there was near panic in the city. Stores were shuttered. There was no bread. It was as if Moscow were in mourning. People descended on Red Square seeking to discover what had happened to the tsar, the center of all authority, the cornerstone of their lives and their society.

Not long afterward, however, two letters from Ivan reached Moscow. Delivered to the new metropolitan, Afanasy, they came from Alexandrova Sloboda, a small town northeast of Moscow, used as a royal residence. In them Ivan announced that he wished to retire from the throne. In the first letter he denounced the actions of the boyars and the clergy, bitterly accusing them of trying to usurp his authority and bring chaos to Moscow. In the second letter, by contrast, Ivan assured the people at large that he harbored no grudge against them but was their friend in seeking to end their oppression by the boyars and the clergy. Ivan asked that this letter be read aloud in Red Square.

The people, horrified by the tsar's announcement, now pleaded with the clergy to entreat their sovereign to return. They wanted to assure Ivan that if he asked they would rise up and destroy his enemies. The bishops were told to implore the tsar to return and rule "as he pleased."

In December 1564 Ivan secretly moved his household
from the Kremlin to Alexandrova Sloboda and threatened
to abdicate unless given a guarantee of absolute power.
The horrified Muscovites sent a delegation of boyars and
clerics to persuade Ivan (right) to return.

Upon returning to Moscow from Alexandrova Sloboda, Ivan began a cruel and vindictive campaign of torture and execution against his enemies, real and imagined. Impalement on a hook was a common form of torture in the Russia of Ivan's day.

With these instructions, Metropolitan Afanasy and his colleagues set out for Alexandrova Sloboda in a solemn procession. First came the monks and priests carrying lighted candles, crosses, and icons. Then came the boyars in their tall hats and long kaftans, the heavy, embroidered robes worn by the nobles. Hundreds of common citizens followed. They found the tsar in a log cabin filled with icons taken from the Kremlin. The throng begged Ivan to return. He promised to think it over and give his answer in a few days.

At length the answer came. It was stern and demanding. Ivan agreed to return to the Kremlin, but first the clergy and boyars had to sign a deed guaranteeing him what amounted to absolute power. The tsar insisted on hunting down and dealing with his enemies as he saw fit, with no questions and no criticism. In addition, Ivan demanded compensation for the cost of moving his household to Alexandrova Sloboda and back.

The unhappy boyars and bishops agreed. Ivan then returned, his fury seemingly increased. Several boyars who had opposed him in the past were quickly executed. Others were arrested and subjected to torture. A British ambassador to Ivan's court described the manner by which guilt or innocence was determined: "The only method of investigation employed is torture, for here one feels obliged to compel the alleged offender to confess his guilt. Without such confession a conviction is impossible. The culprit is whipped with ox nerves or leather lashes as thick as one's finger, which bite into his flesh; or else he is tied to a spit and roasted. Alternatively he may have a rib broken and twisted with red-hot tongs or the flesh beneath his nails may be cut away.

"Capital punishment takes the following forms: hanging, decapitation, bludgeoning, impalement, drowning, freezing under the ice, burning, etc. Often those who are sentenced in summer are kept in custody until the winter so that they may be frozen to death."

The terrible times had begun.

6

The State Within a State

Ivan now was gripped by a mania. It was evident upon his return to Moscow in February 1565 that Ivan had undergone a severe emotional crisis. He suffered from nightmares and hallucinations. His eyes were dulled. His hair and beard had almost fallen out. He saw enemies on all sides, and his fury was terrible. The skepticism and distrust the tsar had previously shown had now grown into acute paranoia.

Shortly after he returned to Moscow from Alexandrova Sloboda the tsar created a special subdivision in the state, the *oprichnina*. The name came from the word *oprich*, which means apart, and the oprichnina became in effect a state within, but apart from, the existing state, or *zemshchina*. The Russian word for land is *zemlya*, and the zemshchina continued to be governed by the landowning boyars.

With the establishment of the oprichnina, Ivan began a wholesale reordering of Russian society. His wrath fell first upon friends and associates of Prince Kurbsky. Individuals who opposed him inevitably

> *The more Ivan oppressed the country, the more he was hated; and the more he felt hated, the more fiercely determined he was to discover those who were plotting against his life.*
> —HENRI TROYAT
> French historian

As part of his drive for absolute power, in 1565 Ivan created a separate state, the *oprichnina*, over which he had complete control.

were executed. Entire families of boyars, including their servants and estate peasants, were ruined and their lands confiscated and given to the officials of the new organization, the *oprichniki*. The confiscations were not carried out blindly. The estates of the boyars close to Moscow were seized and given to lesser nobles who originally had come from distant provinces. The Moscow boyars were in turn sent to colonize wilderness areas in the far north. With Ivan's blessing, the new owners of the Moscow-area estates treated their peasants brutally. By one estimate, they extracted a tenfold increase in their levies on the peasants during this time.

The oprichnina was given its own special royal court, its own ministers, and its own police. Ivan would eventually recruit about 6,000 oprichniki, many of them former bandits, criminals, and itinerant monks. He left the Kremlin to live with this evil crew in an area of Moscow in the Arbat that he had set apart for them. He dragged his sons, Ivan and Fyodor, to live with him there. Later the tsar moved to Alexandrova Sloboda, where he estab-

The broom-and-dog's head insignia on the saddle of the mounted *oprichniki*, the members of the oprichnina, symbolized their orders to sniff out and sweep away corruption. Instead, they frequently committed sadistic crimes without any restraint from Moscow's higher authorities.

NEW YORK PUBLIC LIBRARY PICTURE COLLECTION

lished the oprichnina court and remained for nearly 10 years. At both places he was protected by the oprichniki, whose name was to become a symbol of bestial cruelty. The oprichniki dressed all in black and rode only black horses with black harnesses. A broom and a dog's head were embroidered on a small pennant affixed to the saddles, symbolizing their orders to nose out corruption and sweep it away, but instead of fighting corruption, the oprichniki embodied it. They looted stores and homes; they burned the shops of tradesmen who would not pay extortion money; they raped women prisoners and murdered seemingly at will.

Ivan behaved as badly as any of them. The interest in religion that had marked his youth now took on bizarre trappings. Ivan, dressed as a monk, would harangue his new officials on the necessity of leading moral, upright lives. Then, immediately afterward, he would join them in disgusting orgies. At other times he would personally join his sadistic police in torturing prisoners and then leave them to go to the monastery, where he would beat his head on the floor and beg divine forgiveness. Torture sessions and executions were timed so as not to interfere with church services.

New associates — all oprichniki — came into his life. The most important of them were Malyuta Skuratov, Afanasy Viazemsky, and Aleksei Basmanov and his son, Fyodor. Skuratov was one of the petty boyars from the outskirts of Moscow who had benefited by Ivan's redistribution of estates in the early days of the oprichnina. He quickly became one of Ivan's favorites and by most accounts was involved in many of the worst episodes of this period, including the murder of Metropolitan Philip.

Philip became metropolitan in 1566 when Afanasy fell ill and retired to a monastery. Why Ivan encouraged his election is a mystery, for the new metropolitan was a scrupulously honest, outspoken, deeply religious man who publicly condemned the tsar for the excesses of the oprichnina. Philip often intervened on behalf of prisoners and conducted masses for those executed.

> *Who can teach, who can punish, who can enlighten me, stinking dog that I am? I have ever been prone to drunkenness, lechery, fornication, vileness, murder, theft, rapine, hatred, and every evil.*
> —IVAN THE TERRIBLE

Philip continuously urged the tsar to stop the tortures and murders of his innocent subjects. The vengeful tsar and the headstrong metropolitan quarreled incessantly. On one occasion, in 1568, when Ivan and a force of black-robed oprichniki entered the Uspensky Cathedral in the Kremlin, Philip refused to give Ivan the customary blessing for the tsar, coolly stating, "I do not recognize the Orthodox Tsar in this strange dress, and I do not recognize him in the actions of his government. . . . Fear the judgment of God, O Tsar!" Ivan raced out of the church in a fit of wrath.

Eight months later Ivan ordered Philip arrested and deposed. He was replaced by Metropolitan Kiril, who feared the oprichnina and would remain silent. Basmanov and Skuratov were then turned loose on Philip, whose fate was now sealed. He was not murdered, however, for another year. According to one version of the events, Philip was taken to Alexandrova Sloboda, where he was brutally tortured and hanged on a hook in a cellar. A second version claims that after a long torture an emaciated Philip was smothered or strangled by Skuratov in December 1569.

In the winter of 1567-68 Ivan's police intercepted letters from Polish authorities to several high-ranking boyars urging them to flee to Lithuania. Ivan, with Skuratov's aid, proceeded to annihilate the unfortunate boyars, their wives, children, servants, and even the animals on their estates. The tsar and his henchmen went on an orgy of murder, rape, and pillage for the entire following summer. Ivan himself is reported to have insisted that the best-looking women seized in these raids be kept for him; the others — 500 in all — were allotted to his subordinates to do with as they wanted. The horrors of this time are hard to believe. One of Ivan's favorite diversions was to swoop down on an estate and order his men to cart off the women, who sometimes would be stripped and placed in a fenced-in area with a clutch of chickens. They would then be ordered to chase the chickens while Ivan's soldiers took archery practice, using the darting women as targets. The men of the estate, locked in one of the buildings, would be surrounded with explosives that the oprichniki would then detonate, killing all inside. Ivan was said to take delight in watching the bodies fly.

The most brutal of Ivan's outrages took place in 1570 in the ancient city of Novgorod, approximately 300 miles northwest of Moscow. The incident began, as many others at this time had also begun, with Ivan suspecting the city's inhabitants of treason. The tsar came to believe that the authorities in Novgorod were negotiating with the Poles to sabotage his ongoing war in Livonia.

When Ivan suspected the leaders of Novgorod of treason he and the oprichniki methodically massacred the city's citizens in 1570. A contemporary account estimated the final death toll at 60,000.

At the Cathedral of St. Sophia in Novgorod, Ivan sought Archbishop Pimen's blessing but was refused. Ivan subsequently ordered his men to plunder the cathedral and had the prelate publicly humiliated by stripping him to his underwear and tying him to a horse.

66

The tsar was too cunning to make a frontal assault on the city. Instead he first attacked the monasteries around the city, seizing in all 500 monks, whom he put in irons. Entering the city itself, his oprichniki seized all the prominent merchants and their families. Then the wholesale killing began. First to die were the elders of the church; their mauled bodies were sent back to the monasteries for burial. Having disposed of them, Ivan went next to the Cathedral of St. Sophia, where Archbishop Pimen was waiting. Ivan sought the prelate's blessing. The austere archbishop refused. Ivan denounced him as a traitor but insisted that he conduct mass. The tsar then forced him to attend a state banquet. At the feast, Ivan was in a frenzy. He shouted curses at the archbishop and his aides and ordered his men to plunder the cathedral. Then he had Pimen and the other clergy arrested and taken outside the city. In a bizarre charade, he first humiliated the archbishop before everyone assembled, forcing the clergyman to strip to his underwear and then tying him to a white mare, which trotted off in the direction of Moscow as Pimen strummed a lyrelike instrument. Ivan also ordered the most prominent boyars of Novgorod and their families arrested and brought to him as well. All of them — boyars, priests, wives, families, servants — were tortured mercilessly, wives having to watch the horrors wreaked on their husbands, children watching their parents suffer. They were burned with red-hot irons. They were whipped mercilessly. They were then bound to horses and dragged to the Volkhov River and drowned. Women and children were tied together in bundles and thrown off bridges into the river.

The scale of the Novgorod massacre was unbelievable. From 500 to 1,000 people were executed each day for five weeks, according to a contemporary chronicle, which put the final toll at 60,000 people. Prince Kurbsky, in his own biography of Ivan, puts the toll at 15,000.

After the slaughter, Ivan ordered the surviving men of Novgorod, said to number only 17 in all, to gather before him. He then admonished them, "Men of Novgorod who are left alive, pray God for our religious sovereign power, for victory over all visible and invisible foes." The killing over, Ivan and his oprichniki then looted the monasteries and the homes of the boyars, set fire to the emptied buildings, and left Novgorod. The devastated city never regained the prominence it had enjoyed.

For some months the killing and the looting by the oprichniki continued. No one was immune. In 1569 Ivan even ordered the death of his own cousin Vladimir of Staritsa, together with all his friends and his family. But the day of reckoning was coming, in the form of the Tatar invaders Kurbsky and his men had overcome so many years before. This time, however, Kurbsky was not there to help defend Moscow.

COLLECTION VIOLLET

Ivan (seated) greatly enjoyed the cruel torture and killing of his subjects. His bizarre behavior encouraged the oprichniki to commit similar atrocities.

7

The Wasted Years

Beginning in 1569, Ivan turned on his own creation and launched a terrible purge of the oprichniki. For a short while Skuratov managed to keep the tsar's favor, and the orgies of murder, rape, and pillage continued. By the end of the year Ivan ordered the arrest of Skuratov and the Basmanovs. The oprichnina quickly went into decline, and the black-garbed oprichniki began to disappear. In June 1571 Ivan conducted a second purge, executing many of the remaining prominent oprichniki. The following year Ivan abruptly abolished the hated organization.

But the results of those terrible years were still starkly evident in the country. With the dismemberment of the former great estates close to Moscow and the staggering rents levied by the oprichniki landlords, the local peasants who previously had served the Moscow boyars had been largely uprooted. Many of them sought to avoid starvation by dragging their families into the northern wilderness, where they sought to carve farms out of the forests. Others, willing to risk Tatar raids, fled to the south. To give some idea of the extent of the population movement, a tax survey taken some years later for one district near Moscow showed that

> *Christians are being enslaved, Christendom is being destroyed, and my children are not yet grown up.*
> —IVAN THE TERRIBLE
> defending his refusal
> to abdicate in 1571

The internal turmoil in Ivan's Russia was made worse by a series of armed conflicts with several neighboring states. After 1569 Ivan found himself at war with the Crimean Tatars, Lithuania, Poland, and Sweden.

In 1569 Ivan began a purge of the oprichniki, including one of his former favorites, a petty boyar named Malyuta Skuratov, portrayed (left) in this scene from a 1938 stage play. Skuratov had figured prominently in many of the worst depravities of the oprichniki.

nearly two-fifths of the arable land had been abandoned and that only half of the remainder was under actual production. In the Novgorod region, where Ivan's oprichniki had been more active, only seven percent of the land was being farmed.

The uprooted peasants who fled south from Moscow undoubtedly faced the independent, self-governing bands known as Cossacks. A Tatar word, *kazak* meant "free man" or "adventurer" and was applied to the groups, some Tatar, some Russian or Ukrainian, who roamed the steppes of southern Russia.

The independent Cossack bands had first appeared in the 15th century, when the power of the

THE BETTMANN ARCHIVE

Golden Horde was in decline. By the beginning of the 16th century the rulers of both Moscow and Lithuania were using some Cossacks for frontier military service, but the majority of the Cossacks remained free, in service to no one.

During Ivan's reign four major Cossack groups were developing. The Zaporozhian (Ukrainian) Cossacks, who lived on an island in the lower Dnieper River, maintained a military commune of bachelors: no women were permitted in camp, and it meant death for any man who brought a woman in. The remaining three were the Don, Iaik, and Terek Cossacks, named for the river valleys they inhabited. These groups were predominantly Russian.

Fiercely independent and highly disciplined, the Cossacks lived in democratic societies based on

Ivan abruptly abolished the oprichnina in 1572. The devastation wrought by the oprichniki was so great, however, that in many areas near Moscow peasant farmers simply abandoned their villages, leaving most of the region's arable land unused.

73

The Cossacks were independent bands of peasant-soldiers who roamed southern Russia, sometimes in the service of the tsars. The Zaporozhian Cossacks (portrayed in a 19th-century painting by Ilya Repin) lived as a exclusively male military commune on an island in the Dnieper River.

equal rights. Each man had a vote in the governing assembly, which elected the leader of the "host," or group, called a *hetman* by the Ukrainians, *ataman* by the other Cossacks. The leader presided over the assembly in times of peace, but in war he wielded absolute authority over the entire host.

The Cossacks were especially appealing to fleeing peasants because they refused to return any fugitive subject. The peasants in the north, who were being increasingly bound to the land they worked, sought refuge with and often joined the Cossacks, who made their living hunting, fishing, and raiding, especially the Crimean Tatars. Without the food grown by the peasants and the income from the sale of their produce, the boyars in the north no longer could afford to fulfill their obligations to provide the fighting men for the tsar's army and equip and feed them. The already unpopular Livonian War grew even more detested.

Taking advantage of the turmoil inside Ivan's realm, the Crimean Tatars sought to regain a degree of control over south Russia. In 1569 they had waged a strong campaign to recapture Astrakhan but were unable to do so. Thwarted in that endeavor, they turned north toward Moscow two years later. As the enemy approached the capital, Ivan first barricaded himself, with his family and his treasure, in the Troitsky Monastery (Holy Trinity-St. Sergius Monastery), some 40 miles north of Moscow. As the Tatars reached the city gates, he fled even further, eventually ending up over 350 miles to the north. The bulk of the Russian troops remained tied down by the war in Livonia. The minor force in Moscow, deserted by the tsar, could offer only token resistance. The Kremlin managed to hold out against the invaders, but much of the rest of the city was put to the torch. An English officer who was there at the time described the terrible scene: "The city and the suburbs, thirty miles compass, built mostly of fir and oak timber, were set on fire and burnt within six hours' space, with infinite thousands of men, women and children, burnt, smothered to death." As the fires roared through the capital, the dismal sight of Tatar horsemen driving captives before them appeared on the fields south of Moscow. Altogether an estimated 100,000 prisoners and an immense amount of booty were captured. Encouraged by this success, the Tatars attacked again the following year but could not break through the defense perimeter south of the city.

Ivan's state was floundering. Only by luck had the Tatars not recovered all that had been so perilously won by Kurbsky and the others, while in the northwest only internal political chaos in Poland and Lithuania prevented a military disaster for the Russians in that area as well.

When Ivan had first launched the Livonian campaign in 1558, things had gone well for him. He had recaptured several cities, including Narva and Dorpat, but the campaign then seemed to bog down. He never was able to achieve his main aim of cap-

> *They say there is left no house in the city . . . the people were smothered and burnt ten thick, one lying upon another.*
> —BRITISH EMISSARY
> on the Tatar sacking
> of Moscow

Ivan's prospects in the Livonian campaign were threatened in 1569 when Sigismund II Augustus of Poland
forced Lithuania into an alliance with Poland. Called the
Union of Lublin, the alliance established a united front
against Russia. Shown here is a religious celebration of
the union, which ended Lithuania's independence.

turing the strategic cities of Reval (on the Gulf of Finland, in modern Estonia) and Riga. Moreover, the success that had been achieved ended up working against him: in panic at the Russian advances, Reval allowed itself to be taken under Swedish protection, and Livonia was swallowed up by Poland. Ivan then decided to attack Lithuania in 1563 and managed to overrun a large section of the country, his troops penetrating as far as Vilna, the capital. However, in 1569, Ivan found his Baltic campaign in serious jeopardy when King Sigismund II Augustus of Poland forced Lithuania into a union with Warsaw. The result of the Union of Lublin was that Ivan had to face a united Polish-Lithuanian opposition.

In 1572 Sigismund died, leaving uncertainty about who would replace him on the throne. For a time it seemed possible that Ivan would. Many Poles and Russians favored such a plan, seeing in it a chance to unite in one great Slavic empire.

There were many obstacles to such a scheme. First, Ivan demanded that he be crowned monarch separately of Moscow, Poland, and Lithuania and that Livonia formally become part of Moscow. He also insisted that great swatches of Lithuanian and Polish territory, including Kiev, be ceded to Moscow. Kiev, once the most important city in Russia, held a special significance for Ivan and for most Russians. It was in Kiev, in the late 10th century, that Christianity first came to Russia when Grand Prince Vladimir adopted the Orthodox faith of Constantinople. The second obstacle was religious: Poland was Roman Catholic, but Ivan insisted that he be crowned king of Poland by an Orthodox metropolitan. Finally, France, Austria, and Sweden — the powers of western Europe — as well as Turkey in the south were firmly opposed to the proposed union since it would create a monster at their doorstep. So Ivan was spurned, and in his place the Polish Sejm, or parliament of nobles, in May 1573 chose Henri de Valois. Within a year, however, he gave up the throne and returned to France to assume the French crown after the death of his brother. In 1576

> *You say I am harsh and vengeful. It is true, but ask yourselves against whom I am harsh. I am harsh with those who are harsh with me!*
> —IVAN THE TERRIBLE
> to a representative of the Polish court

After the death of Sigismund II Augustus in 1572, the Polish parliament foundered for several years in its search for a permanent replacement. The nobles eventually chose Stephen Báthory, a Hungarian prince, to be the new Polish king in 1576.

the Sejm chose Stephen Báthory, a Hungarian prince of Transylvania, as the new Polish king. For the Poles it turned out to be a wise choice; for Ivan and Moscow, a disaster.

Starting in 1578, the new Polish king routed Ivan's forces in three brilliant campaigns, regaining most of the territory the Russians had conquered in the previous 20 years. In 1578 the Russians were thoroughly beaten by the Swedes at Wenden, and the following year the Russians lost Polotsk and Smolensk, a key gateway between Moscow and Poland, to Báthory's army. After several further setbacks, Ostrov fell in 1581. At this stage, Ivan was contemplating a counteroffensive when the Polish army approached Pskov, a city on the southern shore of Lake Peipus, near the Gulf of Finland. The Russians succeeded in fending off that attack but lost Narva and its other outlets to the Baltic Sea, including Ivangorod and Koporye. Moscow's aggressive ambitions in the west now were completely checked. Ivan had failed to establish a solid Russian presence on the Baltic Sea. Moreover, his Baltic wars had bled Moscow of money and manpower. The state was exhausted.

The humiliating failure of Ivan's Baltic campaign impelled the tsar to seek allies in Europe. In correspondence with Queen Elizabeth I of England Ivan proposed an Anglo-Russian alliance. He even sought to marry a relative of the queen to strengthen ties between the two countries.

During the 1570s Ivan led a lonely and bitter existence in the Old Palace of the Kremlin where, despite his several marriages, he largely cut himself off from contact with the outside world.

Humiliated by these defeats, Ivan searched for allies. England seemed a likely source, which gave rise to some more of Ivan's singular correspondence. In letters to Queen Elizabeth I of England, Ivan proposed an alliance between their countries; he may even have considered marrying the famous British monarch. When it became clear that marriage to Elizabeth was out of the question, it was suggested that Ivan marry one of her close relatives, and it was at this stage that the possibility of a union with Lady Mary Hastings, Elizabeth's grandniece, was raised. Nothing came of the suggestion, however.

It was a bitter time for Ivan, and he seems to have been extremely despondent. He even spoke of giving up the throne and seeking asylum in England.

The tsar retreated further from reality. He avoided the boyars and his advisers. The great courtyard of the Kremlin, the churches, the palaces with their unending corridors, terrified him. "I am physically and mentally sick," Ivan wrote. "The hurt in my soul and my bodily ills increase day by day; and there is no physician who can cure me! In vain have I waited for someone with whom I might share my troubles, but nobody has come. All have repaid with evil the good that I have shown them. There is no justice in this world. Even tsars cannot find it in their subjects and servants."

Ivan found no comfort for his troubles in his private life. He made several marriages in the 1570s. After the death of Maria Temriukovna in 1569, he had married Maria Sobakina, the daughter of a leading merchant in Tver, in October 1571, but she died two weeks later. By this time, Ivan's oldest surviving son and heir, Tsarevich Ivan, was also seeking a bride. Father and son were married within weeks of each other. In April 1572 Ivan married Anna Koltovskaya, a peasant who had caught his fancy, but he divorced her in May 1575. He sent Anna to a convent, where she would become Sister Darya; she outlived Ivan by many years. The next wife was Anna Vasilchikova. Ivan married her in 1575, but she died in 1577. The next union, that same year, was with a beautiful widow, Vasilisa Melentieva, but the marriage was never recognized by the church. She, too, was eventually sent to a convent. In all his marriages, Ivan never made the strong emotional attachment he had formed with Anastasia.

Ivan appeared to have abandoned further notions of marriage, but the leading boyars and the clergy continued to promote the idea. Only two of Ivan and Anastasia's six children had survived, and one of them, Fyodor, was weak and regarded as simpleminded. The great nobles and bishops wanted a more secure line of succession to the Moscow throne. They were also made uneasy by Ivan's obsession with England, fearing the tsar might even leave Russia. Thus, under pressure from his boyars, in the summer of 1580 Ivan agreed to marry Maria Nagaya, the daughter of a court official. The union would produce one son, Dmitri, born in 1582, but that unfortunate child would do nothing to prolong the Muscovite Rurik dynasty.

> *I do not find her beautiful and I cannot imagine she would be found so by such a connoisseur of beauty as my brother Ivan.*
> —ELIZABETH I
> queen of England, on Lady Mary Hastings

8

The Tragedy of the Two Ivans

Pressure was building on Ivan to make peace with Poland. In July 1581 Pope Gregory XIII sent a special envoy, Antonio Possevino, to try to reconcile Warsaw and Moscow, but the Jesuit seemed more interested in converting the Russians to Catholicism. Ivan refused to consider the issue. "The pope is not Christ," Ivan snorted, "his throne is not a cloud and his bearers are not angels." Yet Ivan seemed to realize he had to end the war. The setbacks in the west provoked among the boyars growing criticism of the tsar's policies. Pskov, besieged by Báthory, bravely held out despite receiving no help from Moscow. Ivan was acutely sensitive to the mounting rumors that he was too old and ineffectual to pursue aggressive action against his enemies. His despondent mood was not lightened by the desire of some of his boyars to have Tsarevich Ivan assume command of the army.

In 1582 Moscow signed a ten-year truce with Warsaw, and in 1583 Moscow concluded a three-year truce with Sweden. Ivan lost all the territory he had gained in the early stages of the war and even had

> *Wretch that I am, I have killed my son!*
> —IVAN THE TERRIBLE

With his leadership ability in question and his policies under fire, Ivan became increasingly paranoid. When his boyars pressured him to appoint his son Ivan to lead the army, Ivan fell into a state of despair that would prove tragic both for his family and his country.

Pope Gregory XIII sent a special envoy to Moscow in 1581 in an effort to negotiate peace between Russia and Poland. Although Ivan rebuffed the envoy, over the next few years he did move to end his unsuccessful military adventures.

THE BETTMANN ARCHIVE

We have not had Roman churches in the past, nor will we have them in the future.
—IVAN THE TERRIBLE
to Possevino, papal legate

to cede a number of other towns to Sweden. Ivan's war — Moscow's first great drive to establish a foothold on the Baltic — had ended in dismal failure. It would be more than a century before Russia's quest for access to the Baltic Sea would be successful.

Tsarevich Ivan was 27 years old at this time and was as headstrong as his father. He had at first been kept somewhat isolated from his father after his mother's death, but later the boy was dragged into his father's rough entourage and the two Ivans became close and constant companions. The similarity of their temperaments, particularly the fierceness of their tempers, was to cause tragedy.

By this time the slightest annoyance could send Tsar Ivan into a blind fury. One day in November 1581 he went to his son's quarters in the palace at Alexandrova Sloboda to collect his son and daugh-

84

In the early 1580s Moscow signed treaties with both Poland and Sweden that ended hostilities. This Russian seal
was affixed to two treaties with Sweden. In a major defeat, Ivan was compelled to withdraw from the Baltic territories he had conquered over the previous 25 years.

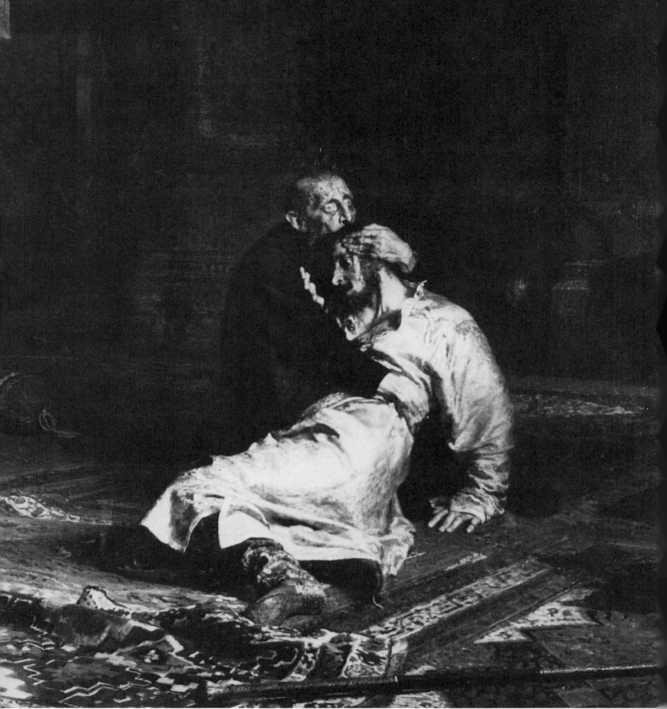

In this painting by Ilya Repin, the dying Tsarevich Ivan is cradled by his distraught father. In 1581 Tsar Ivan, in a fit of anger, struck his son and heir with an iron-tipped staff, killing him. He bitterly mourned the loss for the rest of his life.

ter-in-law for a special religious service. When he got there he found that the daughter-in-law was not dressed in the proper manner. Ivan flew into a rage and began to beat the unfortunate woman, who was pregnant. Hearing his wife's cries, the younger Ivan, who had been in another room, rushed in and tried to restrain his father. That only infuriated Ivan more; to him it was sacrilegious for someone to strike the tsar. The argument apparently ended, for father and son warily withdrew, but the mutual resentment simmered.

It is uncertain exactly what happened when the two Ivans met again later that day. Aside from a young courtier, Boris Godunov, it is unknown who else witnessed the events. When the tsar began to talk of his wealth, a favorite subject, the tsarevich retorted that it was meaningless if the state was not strong enough to hold it. Tsar Ivan interpreted the remark as an assault on his conduct of the war and became enraged. He lashed out at his son with the heavy, iron-tipped staff that he now always carried. Boris Godunov tried to restrain the tsar but was struck down and stabbed with the staff's sharp point. In his fury, Ivan continued to lash out at his son, eventually striking the young man a deadly blow on the temple. Tsar Ivan, in shock and covered with his son's blood, tried to stop the profuse bleeding. The dying tsarevich, barely able to speak, indicated his forgiveness. Ivan descended into an unending grief as his son lingered for a few days, then died.

Remorse now gripped Ivan. He contemplated suicide. One night he left his palace with his surviving son, Fyodor, went outside the Kremlin walls and climbed the bell tower of St. Basil's Cathedral. For a time they tolled the bell. But then Ivan began to howl in grief and tried to fling himself out onto the cobblestones of Red Square far below. Somehow, Fyodor restrained him, and the king fell into an unconscious stupor.

Ivan fully realized the monstrosity of what he had done. The fiery tsar lost his thunder. Ivan would be haunted by his deed for the remainder of his life.

The Bell Tower of Ivan the Great (center) in the Kremlin. Ivan's surviving son, Fyodor, was sickly and feebleminded. He enjoyed spending time in the Kremlin bell towers, where he would listen to the ringing bells for hours.

After the death of his son, the despondent Ivan came to depend heavily upon an aide, Boris Godunov, who, as this portrait indicates, eventually became tsar himself.

He gave up wearing jeweled robes and dressed in simple black. He fell into fits of groaning or uncontrollable weeping. He often had trouble sleeping and feared the disturbing dreams that plagued him.

Ivan also understood the political consequences of his action. Quite apart from murdering his own son, he had once again thrown Moscow into the terrible uncertainty of not knowing who the next ruler would be. Fyodor, the surviving son of Anastasia Romanova, was by all accounts little better than feebleminded. He was devoted to the pomp and circumstance of religion and was especially fond of bell-ringing.

Ivan spoke increasingly of suicide and abdication. At one point he appeared to have decided to relinquish the throne, but the boyars, wary of being branded disloyal should Ivan change his mind, entreated him to remain as tsar. Ivan came to rely more and more on the advice of Godunov, who had quickly recovered from the wounds suffered in trying to protect Tsarevich Ivan. Godunov, an intelligent, resourceful man, was at this time about 30 years of age and was carefully cementing his relationship with the royal family. He would eventually achieve this by marrying his sister to Ivan's surviving son and future tsar, Fyodor.

Godunov, of Tatar origin, was a man of both imposing physical stature and formidable ambition. Although he was intellectually astute and eager to learn new things, Godunov apparently had never learned to read or write. He signed documents by sketching a tiny bird (*godun* is the Tatar word for meadowlark). Godunov was also politically astute. Some years earlier he had married the daughter of the evil but powerful Skuratov, the most infamous of Ivan's colleagues in the oprichnina. When Skuratov fell from Ivan's favor, Godunov managed to stay on good terms with the tsar. He was also close to Nikita Romanov, Anastasia's uncle and one of the leading boyars of the time. Despite these signs of cynical pragmatism, he was also a man of vision. Under his guidance, in the last years of Ivan's reign, Moscow would again turn its eyes to the east.

Day by day, Ivan came to have increasing regard for this handsome young man with the majestic stature and wily brain.
—HENRI TROYANT
French historian, on
Boris Godunov

ЦРЬ І ВЕЛІКІЙ КНЗЬ   ІОЛ ВАСИЛЬЕВИ КСЕЙ РУСИ

9

Founding a New Empire

It was somewhat ironic that the new Russian drive through the Ural Mountains was a direct result of Ivan's unsuccessful attempt to turn Moscow's face to the west. The motivation for the eastward effort stemmed from the need to obtain furs and minerals to trade with the British and Dutch merchants who had come to Moscow under Ivan's protection.

The Siberian fur trade would make many people rich. None profited more than the imperious Stroganov family, who had already done very well for themselves in providing the salt so essential in preserving food in those days before refrigeration.

The Stroganovs, originally a Novgorod family, had begun as merchants along the Dvina River in the 14th century. In Ivan's time the head of the family was wily Anika Stroganov. Actions such as supplying the rich ermines that were sent from Moscow as a present to England's Queen Elizabeth had left him in Ivan's good graces. In return he received greater salt mine concessions. When Ivan felt compelled to ban the production and sale of vodka, it was Anika Stroganov who imported the foreign

> *[Ivan] scarcely lifted a finger and the vast new empire of Siberia fell into his hands.*
> —ROBERT PAYNE and
> NIKITA ROMANOFF
> historians, on the conquest
> of Siberia

During the later years of his reign Ivan reaped the benefits of Russian eastward expansion. The exploitation of the rich resources in the Ural Mountains and the conquest of Siberia brought the tsar added wealth and land.

wines that the gentry drank instead. Nor was the tsar the Stroganovs' only friend in high places; Anika's son Yakov, who was something of a physician, helped repair Boris Godunov's wounds when he lay near death after trying to prevent the tsar from murdering his son.

Ivan had long seen Siberia, the vast lands east of the Ural Mountains, as a Russian preserve. His grandfather had established friendly ties with the Siberian khan in Tyumen, who, in turn, had been an ally of the Russians against the Golden Horde in 1480. In 1558 Ivan had awarded Anika Stroganov an enormous tract of land around Perm on the Kama River in the western foothills of the Urals. In addition, Stroganov was given permission by the tsar to colonize the land by inviting immigrants and those peasants whose names did not appear on the existing land registers for western Russia to settle

Russian ambassadors to Germany in 1576. Ivan's efforts to expand trade connections in Europe were made considerably easier by the abundance of valuable furs and minerals from Siberia.

there. Nine years later Ivan sent an expedition of Cossacks to explore Siberia and report on its resources. They returned with rough sketch maps, which were to form the basis of later expeditions and land grants. The most prominent of such grants was one given to Anika Stroganov's sons Grigori and Yakov in 1574. For a term of 20 years, Ivan permitted them to mine copper, zinc, lead, and sulphur and collect furs from what was called "the Siberian Ukraine," a huge expanse beyond the Urals along the Tobol River.

The Stroganovs built forts in the Urals to protect their people and goods, but several skirmishes with the Tatar forces of Kuchum, khan of Sibir, convinced the merchant family that the Siberian khanate had to be eliminated. The Stroganovs appealed to the tsar for help. Ivan gave them his approval and blessing but refused to send aid.

The conquest of Siberia was the fruit of the vision and enterprise of the Stroganovs and of the courage and fortitude of a small band of Cossacks.
—IAN GREY
British historian

Yermak, a Don Cossack and veteran of Ivan's Livonian campaign, was chosen by the wealthy Stroganov merchant family to defeat the khan of Siberia. With a private army of only 800 men, he was able to nearly double the size of the Russian empire.

The Stroganovs decided to finance an expedition on their own. They found a ready and willing lieutenant to lead it in the person of a Don Cossack from the Kama River region. His name was Yermak, and he had fought without great zeal or distinction in Ivan's Livonian campaigns. Now he had returned to his native area and had risen to be a man of some eminence among the Cossacks. However, his fame derived from his success at brigandage, even to the extent of hijacking the tsar's vessels carrying supplies down the Volga River. He had also spent some time in the service of the Stroganovs and had a firsthand knowledge of the riches and risks that were to be found in Siberia.

In September 1581 Yermak and about 800 men crossed the Urals and entered Siberia. They had no horses — the steep mountain passes and dense forests were largely impenetrable by horse — but were provided with muskets and a few cannon. They had

barely made it through the Urals when winter fell and they were forced to wait for spring in the area where the city of Tyumen now stands. In May 1582 they started forward again, this time reaching the Tobol River. Throughout the summer there were numerous skirmishes between Yermak's little army and the Tatars, who greatly outnumbered them. Finally, in October 1582, after an adroit display of military cunning, Yermak succeeded in capturing the Tatar capital of Iskir (Sibir). Khan Kuchum and his nephew Mahmetkul fled in panic, but Mahmetkul was soon taken prisoner. A jubilant Yermak sent a trusted aide to Moscow to tell the tsar the good news that Russian dominance of Siberia east to the Ob and Irtysh Rivers and north to the Arctic was now secure. To reinforce the point, Yermak sent along 2,400 priceless sable furs, 50 beaver pelts, and 50 black fox skins. On receiving the news and the gifts, Ivan was exultant. Together with the capture

After he captured the Tatar capital of Iskir in October 1582, Yermak sent emissaries bearing priceless furs to Ivan's court to announce the good news. In his jubilation, Ivan had Yermak elevated to the nobility, but the Cossack died in Siberia before he could make his victorious journey to Moscow.

The traditional right of Russian estate peasants to move was abolished by Ivan in 1581; the peasants were now serfs, bound to the estates on which they were born. The measure was designed to provide a permanent labor force for a new class of landowner whom Ivan hoped would be more loyal to him.

THE BETTMANN ARCHIVE

of Kazan, the conquest of Siberia doubled the size of Ivan's state. Yermak, the lowborn former outlaw, was raised to the nobility. He did not enjoy his new status for long, however; he died in an ambush in August 1584, drowning while attempting to escape across the Irtysh River in full armor.

Even as the Russians were moving to colonize and subjugate the wild areas of Siberia, Ivan was occupied closer to home with solidifying the new social order that had been introduced during the oprichnina.

In his early years — before the formation of the oprichnina — he seems to have been genuinely intent on achieving some fairness in the state's dealings with its people. This was the reason for his granting of the right of petition to the crown for the redress of civil or criminal wrongs on the part of the tsar's governors and the establishment of the right of certain districts to decide the way in which taxes were levied and collected. The desire to achieve some wider representation of the opinion of the state's citizens was shown in Ivan's summoning of the assembly of the land, the Zemsky Sobor, in 1550 and especially in 1566 when the nobles, the clergy, the landowners, the merchants, and even some wealthier peasants were asked to take part in the discussion of the war in Livonia.

But Ivan was determined to prevent the Russian boyars from gaining power to the extent that they would repeat the anarchic situation in Poland, where the great nobles not only controlled the election of the monarch but had a virtual veto power over any of his decisions. The brutal campaign that had been directed at trying to break the power of the great boyars was also designed to firmly establish a new class of landowner, called a *pomestchik*, whose situation was dependent on faithful service to the tsar. In 1581 Ivan made a new gesture to further bind these new squires to his cause: he provided them with a permanent labor force.

Until this time the peasants who lived on the estates were to all intents and purposes free men. There were some restrictions; for instance, they could move from the estate where they had been living and working to another estate only following the harvest in the fall. Now even that right was taken from the peasants; they had to remain where they had been born and would from then on be regarded as serfs, bound to the estate they worked. This bond was further reinforced by debt. Most peasants had to borrow from the landowner for their basic housing and farming needs. The funds to buy a cow or build a house were borrowed from the landowner, and seldom could the debt ever completely be paid off. The serf did retain some rights. He could sue in court to redress a wrong. He could also own land and indeed could have serfs of his own but as a practical matter this seldom happened. Technically, these peasants were not slaves — they were not pieces of property, owned by the nobleman — but in reality they were treated as such. Ivan's absolutist rule, a system of dictation from above, had reached down to the lowest rung of society. The roots of Russian autocracy were firmly embedded.

Their obligations undefined, the serfs were at the mercy of the landlords who came to exercise increasing judicial and police authority on their estates.
—NICHOLAS V. RIASANOVSKY
Russian historian, on serfdom

10

Death of a Tyrant

By the winter of 1583–84, it had been half a century since young Ivan had succeeded his father on the throne in Moscow, and it had been nearly 40 years since he had actively assumed power as tsar. In that long period he had transformed the country from a collection of petty fiefdoms into a true national state, and he brought Russia into the wider European arena. Russia had been forcibly united under the central power of a ruling autocrat through the fierce subjugation of Novgorod and Pskov and the determined drive south along the Volga River and through the Ural Mountains into Siberia. Ivan's simultaneous lunge westward toward the Baltic had failed and would not be successfully renewed until the time of Peter the Great, but he had brought Moscow into greater contact with the ideas and inventions of western Europe, and the trade ties he had cemented with the Dutch and the English would persist long after his death.

In his long reign Ivan had suffered many tragedies and disappointments. The deaths of his first wife, Anastasia, and of five of his seven children, especially his own murder of Tsarevich Ivan, had been crushing events. They had reinforced the already morbid nature of the tsar, and in his final years he

> *No monarch ever made a more uncompromising claim to divine right than did Ivan the Terrible.*
> —MELVIN C. WREN
> American historian

Suffering from numerous physical ailments and the mental anguish resulting from the deaths of his beloved first wife and his eldest son, Ivan (seated) had become convinced by 1584 that his death was imminent.

was preoccupied with relinquishing the power and obligations of his office.

As the winter wore on, Ivan's physical and mental condition deteriorated further. His body, particularly his legs and his genitals, were horribly swollen because of dropsy and other ailments. Even the tsar knew that he could not last much longer. Mysterious omens seemed to confirm that likelihood.

One evening the tsar went out onto the Red Porch of the Kremlin Palace. To his surprise he noticed

An illustration of common medieval superstitions. As Ivan's mental and physical condition grew worse, his belief in superstition and sorcery became stronger. The ailing tsar believed that comets and black birds were omens foretelling his death.

low in the sky, seeming to hang between the Cathedral of the Assumption and the bell tower of Ivan the Great, a comet with a tail shaped like a cross. Ivan was thunderstruck. "This sign foretells my death," he exclaimed. It was reported that a huge black bird appeared every night, flying over the city, cawing maliciously and obviously portending a great evil.

Ivan had always been a strange mixture of Christian and pagan, and toward the end of his life both religions were brought into play. To try to divine his future, he had one of his palace aides send to distant Lapland, far in the north, for women who were supposed to possess great powers of sorcery. In a short time, the seeresses were brought to the Kremlin, where they proceeded to cast spells, search the skies for omens, and commune with their pagan gods. Although Ivan was not told of their findings, they forecast that the tsar's life would end on March 18, 1584.

Ivan grew weaker, and on March 10 he decided not to receive a Lithuanian delegation that had been on its way to Moscow. The envoys were instructed to wait outside the city. On the same day, Ivan sent a long and prayerful letter to an order of monks especially esteemed for their piety. In his letter he said that the tsar "bows to your feet and prays, kneeling before your holiness, begging you to favor him . . . that I may be granted recovery from my present mortal illness and made well."

But, just in case his prayers did not succeed, Ivan the realist made out his will. It was a long document, full of self-deprecation and self-admonition. It named his son Fyodor as the heir to the throne of Moscow. To the infant Dmitri he bequeathed the principality of Uglich on the Volga. Ivan realized that neither the simpleminded Fyodor nor the baby Dmitri was capable of ruling alone, so the will named four of his advisers to the Council of Regents, which would administer the realm. The regents were Ivan Shuisky, Nikita Romanov, Ivan Mstislavsky, and Boris Godunov. They were instructed to look after Ivan's children and to try to keep the nation at

He had nothing but mockery and impatience for his monkish, timorous son.
—HANS VON ECKARDT
German historian, on Ivan's opinion of his successor, Fyodor

Ivan the Terrible died on March 18, 1584, after a long illness. He had spent his last days preparing his will, inspecting the royal treasury, and naming a Council of Regents to rule the country after his death.

peace, particularly with Moscow's Christian neighbors. The draining effects of the long wars with Poland, Lithuania, and Sweden were offered as an example. Ivan did not want them repeated.

Ivan, however, still had some sparks of life. He still liked women, and when Fyodor's beautiful wife, Irina Godunova, entered his bedroom to check on his condition he tried to grab her. She ran from the room, screaming. Ivan also loved to be carried on his chair to inspect the royal treasury. There he would gaze longingly at the diamonds, rubies, pearls, opals, sapphires, and gold. Sometimes he would inspect an especially valued object, said to be the horn of a unicorn, for which he had paid 70,000 marks to a German family. Perhaps his favorite object in the treasure house was the lodestone, a piece of magnetized rock. In Ivan's day it was regarded as magical, and he loved to touch needles to its surface and then string them together by their magnetized points.

On March 18 Ivan felt better. He took a hot bath to ease the discomfort caused by his swollen limbs and ordered that the Lithuanian delegation, which had been stalled in Mozhaisk, start on its way to the capital. Later in the day he took some medicine that had been prescribed. Then he took another bath and, feeling much better, was dressed in a loose kaftan, shirt, and hose. Seeking amusement, he told one of his courtiers, Rodion Birkin, to fetch a chessboard. According to Jerome Horsey, an Englishman at the Russian court, Ivan could not get his king to stand properly on the square. He grew frustrated and fell back on the bed. At first those around him were not unduly alarmed. He had often had similar fainting spells when he was angry, but when the tsar did not revive, they checked him and, as Horsey said, found him "strangled and stark dead."

Godunov promptly took charge. The regents had already formulated the plan for the transfer of power upon the tsar's death. The Kremlin gates were ordered closed. Godunov ordered the streltsy put on alert and the artillery readied on the Kremlin walls

> *Most historians have condemned him as a cruel tyrant, perverted by power. But in the Soviet Union he has been recognized as a great Tsar . . . a national hero.*
> —IAN GREY
> British historian

Ivan's son Fyodor succeeded his father as tsar, but Russia's de facto ruler was Boris Godunov. Godunov had earlier arranged the marriage of his sister to Fyodor, thereby strengthening his own claim to the throne.

for any possible disturbances. As a final measure of protection, the treasury was sealed.

At the same time, Ivan's body was shaved and its hair trimmed. The dead tsar, according to custom, was dressed in a monk's robe and taken through the ritual of admission to a monastic order.

There was some difficulty at first in locating Fyodor to tell him that his father was dead and that he would be the new tsar. Eventually he was found in one of the bell towers, listening in fascination as the bells tolled for his late father. Brought to the room where Ivan lay, the simple young man wept bitterly.

After the full pomp and circumstance of the Orthodox church and the Moscow monarchy had run its course, Ivan was entombed in the Cathedral of Michael the Archangel in the Kremlin. His sarcophagus was placed next to that of Ivan, the son he had murdered three years earlier.

Ivan was gone, but Moscow and Russia would never be the same. Terrible though his reign and his actions had been, he would pass into legend as a strong man for a time when a strong man had been needed. He would serve as a model for future

Russian tsars, especially Peter the Great, who greatly admired Ivan.

The Rurik dynasty virtually died out with Ivan, for Fyodor never was in control and died without heirs in 1598. Ivan's other son, Dmitri, had died earlier under mysterious circumstances. Reports circulated that Boris Godunov had murdered Dmitri in order to assume the throne himself. Godunov did indeed become tsar, ruling from Fyodor's death to his own in 1605.

Godunov's death, reportedly a suicide, plunged Russia into the chaos of the *smutnoe vremya* (literally, the "sad time"), known in English as the Time of Troubles. From the dynastic struggles of this period of civil war finally emerged the family that would rule Russia for 300 years — until the end of the Russian monarchy itself. In 1613, 16-year-old Mikhail Romanov assumed the throne and title of Ivan the Terrible — "Tsar and Autocrat of All Russia." Though Ivan had shaken the Russian state to the core, Muscovite absolutism prevailed, and Russia was left a legacy of autocracy.

During Ivan's reign, all power in the country was centered in him. Ivan the Terrible served as a model for later Russian rulers, including Peter the Great and Stalin, who saw him as a strong, decisive leader. He left to Russia a permanent legacy of autocracy.

Further Reading

Eckardt, Hans Von. *Ivan The Terrible,* trans. by Catherine Alison Phillips. New York: Alfred A. Knopf, 1949.

Graham, Stephen. *Ivan the Terrible: The Life of Ivan IV of Russia.* New Haver.: Yale University Press, 1933.

Grey, Ian. *Ivan The Terrible.* Philadelphia: J. B. Lippincott, 1964.

Lamb, Harold. *The March of Muscovy: Ivan The Terrible and the Growth of the Russian Empire, 1400–1648.* New York: Doubleday & Co., 1948.

Payne, Robert, and Nikita Romanoff. *Ivan The Terrible.* New York: Thomas Y. Crowell, 1975.

Platonov, S. F. *Ivan The Terrible,* ed. and trans. by Joseph L. Wieczynski. Gulf Bridge, FL: Academic International Press, 1974.

Troyat, Henri. *Ivan the Terrible,* trans. by Joan Pinkham. New York: E. P. Dutton, 1984.

Chronology

Aug. 25, 1530	Ivan born to Grand Duke Vasili III of Muscovy and Yelena Glinskaya
1533	Vasili III dies
1538	Princess Yelena dies; beginning of the Shuisky regency
1543	Ivan orders Andrei Shuisky killed
Jan. 16, 1547	Crowned Tsar and Autocrat of All Russia
Feb. 3, 1547	Marries Anastasia Romanova
June 1547	Moscow burns
1548	Ivan establishes Chosen Council
1550	Summons the Zemsky Sobor (assembly of the land)
1552	Defeats the Kazan Tatars
Oct. 1552	Tsarevich Dmitri born
March 1553	Ivan falls ill; succession controversy
June 1553	Tsarevich Dmitri dies
1553	Richard Chancellor arrives in Moscow; establishes British trade interests in Russia
1554	Tsarevich Ivan born
1558	Ivan's third son, Fyodor, born Russian army invades Livonia
Aug. 7, 1560	Tsarina Anastasia dies
1560	Aleksei Adashev dies; Archpriest Sylvester exiled
1564	Prince Andrei Kurbsky, Ivan's most accomplished general, flees Russia
Dec. 1564	Ivan renounces the throne; returns after entreaties of delegation of boyars and princes
Feb. 1565	Establishes a separate court, the oprichnina
1570	Novgorod massacre
May 1571	Moscow sacked by Tatars
1572	Ivan dissolves oprichnina
1573	Solicits Polish crown
1582–83	End of Livonian campaigns
1581–82	Conquest of Siberia
Nov. 19, 1581	Ivan murders his eldest son, Tsarevich Ivan
March 18, 1584	Ivan dies

Index

Thomas Butson has been assistant news editor of *The New York Times* since 1968. A former assistant managing editor of *The Toronto Star*, he covered Pierre Trudeau's political emergence and rise to power. He is also the author of *Gorbachev* and *Trudeau* in the Chelsea House series WORLD LEADERS—PAST & PRESENT.

Arthur M. Schlesinger, jr., taught history at Harvard for many years and is currently Albert Schweitzer Professor of the Humanities at City University of New York. He is the author of numerous highly praised works in American history and has twice been awarded the Pulitzer Prize. He served in the White House as special assistant to Presidents Kennedy and Johnson.